Everyday Innovator
4 Powerful Habits to Cultivate Team Creativity

Christian Byrge, PhD

BIS Publishers

BIS Publishers

Borneostraat 80-A

1094 CP Amsterdam

The Netherlands

T +31 (0)20 515 02 30

bis@bispublishers.com

www.bispublishers.com

ISBN 978 90 636 9681 8

Category: Design / Personal Development / Creativity

Copyright © 2023 Christian Byrge and BIS Publishers.

Affiliation: Vilnius University Business School, Lithuania

International distributor: Hachette

Design by Peter Johnsen

Layout by Henrik Engedal

Copy editing by Celina Mina

Proofreading by McKenna Stroud and Lisbeth Agerskov Christensen

All web references were correct at the time of going to press.

Contents

Introduction

This book is the result of more than fifteen years of dedicated applied research. Fifteen years of experimenting, testing, and analyzing effective innovative processes, extraordinary creativity professionals, and influential innovative teams. Studying how to solve complex problems with breakthrough novel solutions. Investigating how to develop innovative skills and boost creative confidence.

In my search for insights into creativity, I have visited creativity scholars and experts from all over the world, read more than a thousand publications on creativity, conducted more than forty experiments on creativity, and delivered more than three hundred creativity workshops and keynotes involving more than a hundred thousand people.

As an internationally recognized scholar, I have delivered training on creativity in all sorts of contexts, including manufacturing, sales, management, communication, project management, teaching, boards of directors, quality control, innovation, product and service design, entrepreneurship, logistics, business development, and much more. I have delivered keynote speeches, training, and projects across Europe, Asia, and the United States in industries such as shipping, banking, medicine, retail, national defense, public health, education, beer and fruit beverages, oil and gas, zoological gardens, transportation, people in need, clean water, and much more.

As a full professor and global consultant in the field of business creativity, my passion is to help individuals and teams become far more creative in their everyday work and lives.

This book is *easy to read* and *easy to apply,* providing a research-based source of inspiration to kick-start your creativity journey. I hope it will inspire you and your team to develop powerful innovative skills and boost your creative confidence, so you can succeed in more ambitious creative efforts.

Book Structure

The book is structured around the following six sections:

The *Introduction* presents some of the most valuable effects of creativity. You will understand how creativity is the engine for innovation, how it leads to better decisions, and how it is a skill set for the future. You will learn how creativity can be enhanced by implementing reward structures for creative efforts, innovative process methods, as well as nurturing of creative skills and creative confidence. In addition, you will learn about idea systems for collecting, evaluating, and selecting new ideas.

Explore New Grounds takes you through the fundamentals of identifying a problem with high innovative potential. You will learn how to challenge what everyone else takes for granted. This will be a continuous source of starting points for your creative efforts.

Imagine Novel Ideas delves into the production of novel, valuable, and inspiring ideas. You will learn how to imagine new ideas that have the potential to set new standards for your team and industry. This will help you create a foundation upon which you can make better decisions.

Visionary Thinking explains how to evaluate new ideas with a curious, open mind. You will learn to see potential where others can only find trouble. This will help you have a learning perspective when presented with new ideas.

Persuasive Idea Presentation covers some of the most important reflections needed for gaining support and compliance for your new ideas. You will learn how to prepare your idea presentation more persuasively. This will help make the difference between you being considered a weirdo and a genius when presenting your new ideas!

Kick-Start Your Creativity Journey is a whole new world for most people. You will learn how to prepare your creativity journey, how to practice your creative skills, how to boost your creative confidence, how to support the integration of creativity in your daily work tasks, and how to set expectations for creative efforts. This will help you develop the four powerful creative habits that can turn you into a serious innovator and turn your team into an idea machine.

The Power of Creativity

It comes as a surprising insight out of nowhere.

You just know when the idea is right.

It creates motivation, hope, and perseverance. This is exactly what you need to implement the new idea. To replace a declining idea from your daily life, work, industry, or society.

It may be a brilliant idea about a new type of breakfast.

It may be a fun idea about how to invite guests to your wedding.

It may be a novel idea about how to conduct your meetings in a more meaningful way.

It may be a valuable idea about how to communicate with your users.

It may be a breakthrough idea that changes how we all treat animals.

It's fun coming up with wild ideas. Ideas that may defy your team's and industry's current logic. These ideas bring about laughter, imagination, and inspiration. This is exactly what you need for your team to work together to experiment and implement your new ideas.

Creativity has the potential to bring together diverse and opposing views. The potential to turn these into a series of more holistic ideas.

The most important effect from creativity may be in terms of your social relations. You get to know a completely new side of your spouse, children, colleagues, customers, and friends. You see them as creative human beings. You experience being creative together. You feel the energy from their new insights. Suddenly, you know how you can create inspiring new things together.

Better Decisions

Can quantity lead to quality? There are a few areas of life where this holds true.

Most people tend to understand them as opposites. If you want high quantity, you get lower quality. If you go for high quality, you get less quantity.

However, for knowledge, the relation seems to be true. Also, for experience. More knowledge and experience can lead to better decisions. Or rather, they lead to a better foundation for decision-making. You will find it hard to make qualified decisions if you have no knowledge or experience in a particular area.

Imagine you just started a new sport, like surfing. You have never tried surfing before. You have no experience. Your knowledge about surfing comes mainly from watching movies about surfers. Therefore, your foundation for decision-making is quite limited. You may go surfing at beaches with bad waves. You may go surfing in dangerous waters. And you may find it difficult to catch the waves with your surfboard.

So, you book a practice session with a skilled surfer to gain some experience. And you start observing and talking to other surfers. You may even read a few books about surfing. As you gain more experience and knowledge, you gain a better foundation for making decisions. You now know which type of beach to choose. You now know how to check if the water is right. You now know how to catch a wave.

Creativity is strongly connected to knowledge and experience. Once you try out a new idea, it becomes experience. You gain experience with the new idea. As the idea is verified, it turns into knowledge. As such, ideas are the seeds of new experiences and new knowledge.

That may explain why quantity and quality are positively related when it comes to creativity. What does that mean?

Do you stop your creative efforts once you have a viable solution? Do you stop looking for more alternative ideas once you get an idea you like? You are not the only one.

Most people will settle for the first great idea. However, this is an alarmingly clear indication that you have potential for improving your creative skills and confidence. Having just a few good ideas and one great idea will give you a strong belief that this great idea is superior. You essentially evaluate the great idea against the average ideas.

Having several great ideas makes it easier to see the nuances of each great idea. How are the great ideas different from each other? What are the unique values of one great idea over another great idea? How may one great idea be easier to implement than another great idea?

The more novel and valuable the ideas, the better the foundation for decision-making. As such, creativity is a form of business intelligence—a business creativity intelligence. While traditional business intelligence is based on multiple historical data, business creativity intelligence is based on multiple qualified hunches for the future. In other words, creativity helps you make better decisions.

Engine for Innovation

Some ideas make life easier. Others make your work more effective. And then you have those ideas that have innovative potential. These are the truly original ideas. The kind of ideas that cause you to step into an unknown future.

Creativity is often considered to be the engine for innovation. Being creative, you dare to challenge and replace declining ideas with new original solutions. To challenge what everyone else takes for granted.

Creativity makes you think bigger. You get the confidence to dig deeper into complex problems that most others would rather leave as is. And you imagine new uses of technology, especially the type of technologies that follow an exponential development curve for performance and price.

Imagine programmable robot arms will soon cost as little as a new jacket. Now think up situations where robot arms could take over a human task or provide new value. Could such robot arms be used in new ways in supermarkets? In hairdresser salons? In schools? At your work?

Original ideas have the potential to ignite innovation. It is the key ingredient that spurs innovative activities, innovative solutions, and innovative products. These ideas can lead to unforeseen competitive advantages.

They can help advance your current business model. Novel ideas can even lead to new business models that change the dynamic of your industry. You may end up becoming an industry platform which your current competitors would pay to access. Or you may develop a more direct relationship with your end-customers.

Novel ideas have the potential to change organizations and entire industries. They may even lead to new opportunities that go beyond what you ever imagined. Such new competitive advantages often come with unique entry barriers that allow you to have a higher profit margin than your competitors.

Skills for the future

Creativity is increasingly considered one of the most important skills of the near future. It's not just creativity—it's the production of novel ideas that becomes more important.

Are you able to produce novel ideas on command? Can you produce unique ideas at will? Ideas that most people are not likely to come up with?

We see a lot of standard work tasks being taken over by artificial intelligence, robots, machines, and computer software. Creativity seems to be one of the few skills that distinguish humans from all these new machines and technologies that enter your workplace. Soon, it may be one of the few things that cannot be taken over by artificial intelligence.

Creativity will challenge the dominance of IQ as a status symbol. A new IQ 2.0 will emerge. IQ is about being able to identify, understand, and follow existing ideas. It may be a pattern, theory, mathematical formula, or a way of doing something. Creativity is about being able to challenge existing ideas, imagine new and better ideas, and inspire others to follow these new ideas. You may need to separate creativity from IQ. You may need a new symbol of intelligence. A creativity quotient: CQ.

Creativity tests already exist. They are increasingly being used as part of job interviews and corporate development. You may be asked to perform a creativity test for your next job interview. This is increasingly likely if you consider applying for a job related to innovation, business development, or corporate entrepreneurship.

Creativity is becoming increasingly important across all kinds of professions. It not only brings about new ideas for innovation, but it also leads to passion for your work and perseverance for making an impact.

As a creative, you can design your own life. You can change communities, teams, and industries. Creatives are among the most influential in human history. Creatives come up with new ideas and inspire others to follow.

Creatives have done this in science, technology, medicine, service, production, retail, leadership, strategy, sports, communication, economy, construction, health care, and every other part of society and daily life.

As a creative, you can help solve problems faced (and often created) by humanity. You can help push humanity forward.

Time to Be Creative

Employees and leaders are increasingly asked to be innovative. You may also be asked to contribute with your creative ideas for the innovative activities in your organization.

You may be asked to find time for being creative. This may be during facilitated brainstorming sessions or innovative workshops. It also happens during more formal meetings where anything from a few minutes to several hours may be reserved for finding creative solutions. You may also be expected to come up with creative ideas on your own during your everyday work tasks. Perhaps your employer is asking for more innovative solutions or new perspectives on urgent problems.

Do you know how to be creative on command or at will? To be creative, you must simply know how to be creative. What if you don't know? How effective will your creativity sessions be if no one knows how to be creative? If you don't know how to be creative, you are not likely to spend this time in a valuable way.

Maybe you know how to participate in a brainstorming session. But what if your brainstorming session does not lead you to the new insightful ideas you were hoping for? What do you do next? Or what if you must come up with innovative ideas of your own? How will you go about this?

You may feel uncomfortable—or even incompetent—during these creative efforts. Your mind may wander off to more comfortable activities like checking the news, answering emails, or chatting about other matters with your colleagues.

Let's look at this from another perspective. Instead of being asked to be creative, imagine you're asked to spend time playing the violin. Think about a meeting where you are asked to spend time playing the violin. If you know how to play the violin, you will be able to play lovely melodies. But anyone who doesn't know how to play the violin may sound more like an injured animal's cry for help. It will feel like a complete waste of time. Eventually, you may be irritated by the horrible sound and agree to stop the nonsense.

The same is the case with creativity. It's not enough to set aside time to be creative. If you don't know *how* to be creative, it will feel like a waste of time.

You may produce some ideas you have thought or heard of before. These ideas may have been shared with colleagues several times over the years, making you feel like you are doing nothing meaningful. So, you will quickly stop this nonsense also.

Put more simply, those who do not know how to be creative will find no value in using their time to do so. And they will experience their creative efforts as a failure, thus lowering their creative confidence even further.

It is not enough to set aside time for creativity. You must nurture the necessary creative skills so that you know *how* to be creative. You must also develop the creative confidence that you know you will succeed when being creative—that when you set aside time to be creative, you know how to efficiently and successfully develop inspiring new ideas.

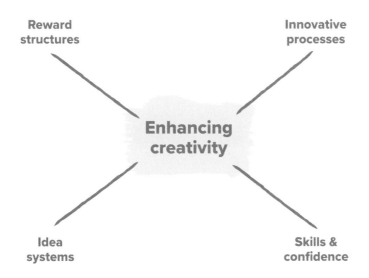

It's worth considering four fundamental approaches for enhancing creativity:

→ Integrating innovative processes
→ Setting reward structures for creative efforts
→ Establishing idea systems
→ Nurturing creative skills and confidence

These four approaches will be presented separately. However, try not to think of them as alternative approaches. Rather, think about them as complementary approaches. Individually, each of them will have positive effects on your creativity. However, it would be better to apply multiple or all four approaches if you want to become significantly more creative.

Innovative Processes

Imagine gathering a team of friends or colleagues. You set aside a couple of hours or more. You give the group a complex problem to solve. What do you expect will happen?

You might succeed in coming up with a brilliant new solution for the problem. However, there is a risk that you may end up spending most of your time discussing what to do, how to do it, when to do it, and who will do it.

One may suggest a collective discussion. Another may want to go for a walk and talk in pairs. One may suggest meditating. You may start discussing whether you should go to an innovation lab. Some may start questioning why you are doing it at all. You may not be able to agree on which idea to choose. This can lead to a never-ending, meaningless discussion. Eventually, you risk not being able to come up with a solution at all.

The concept of the innovative process is to provide a method that answers all the why, what, how, when, where, and who questions. Theory or anecdotes will explain why the innovative process method will work. Step-by-step instructions will detail what exactly to do during the innovative process. A creativity tool kit will guide how to be creative. A framework will show how much time is needed for each step and for the entire process. Advice will inspire where to perform the innovative process, and what type of interior and materials are needed. The method will also instruct who to invite into the innovative process.

An innovative process provides a structure for your creative efforts. It facilitates your team through a series of steps that are designed to stimulate problem understanding, idea development, idea evaluation, and idea testing. As a result, your team will be able to direct their collective attention toward being creative together. It makes your creative efforts more effective, helping you succeed at coming up with more novel, valuable, and feasible ideas.

The innovative process is often facilitated as a workshop involving several steps and iterations. They are well prepared and planned for a specific date and time. For example, on Wednesday from 10:00 a.m. until 6:00 p.m.

Innovative processes are generally planned as a group activity. Almost every famous innovative process method is designed for creativity to be a team activity. Those looking for structured individual innovative process methods may not be able to find them easily.

You may know about innovative processes from the countless brainstorming sessions that have been organized in and across teams since the 1950s. You may also have come across some of its other names like Design Thinking, Google Sprints, and Creative Problem Solving (CPS).

The innovative process may currently be the most popular approach for enhancing creativity. It is widely used in and across companies, public organizations, and educational institutions. Innovative processes are so popular that many teams use them as their only approach to creativity.

Innovative processes are effective in making short-term enhancement of creativity. They successfully bring together diverse groups of people to creatively tackle the same problem for a predefined period.

However, this is also their greatest weakness: it's temporary. When the innovative process is over, creativity stops. Afterward, you go back to your normal "non-creative" way of working.

Innovative processes are not designed to develop skills and confidence. Their main purpose is to facilitate teams to temporarily enhance creative efforts.

Therefore, innovative processes are highly valuable in organizations where creative efforts should be targeted toward specific problems at specific times, during specific work tasks or projects. Conversely, innovative processes are less valuable in organizations where creative efforts are expected to be an integrated part of everyday work.

Idea Systems

"We already have enough ideas. We just need to find them." Where are they? Who comes up with these ideas? Are they written on Post-it notes somewhere? Are they waiting in desk drawers? Waiting to be discovered? Are they shared at the coffee machine? Or during lunch?

You get ideas all the time. Maybe you don't get great ideas all the time. But you definitely get good ideas sometimes. What if you collected all your ideas? If you were somehow able to put them into a collective idea box? Then you would be able to evaluate all your ideas systematically against each other and make better decisions regarding which ideas to pursue.

The famous idea box. **For decades, it has been popular to systematically collect, evaluate, and select ideas.** Modern technology has revolutionized how ideas are collected. Digital idea boxes make it easier to collect and elaborate on ideas in real time during meetings, workshops, and everyday work tasks.

The notion of the idea system is to make ideas that already exist in your organization a point of departure. As you perform your daily work tasks, you naturally stumble into new ideas. They come as you get irritated by some standard work procedure. They come while you drive home from work. Or you get them at a social gathering while listening to how things are run at your friend's workplace.

How do you collect all these ideas? You may use weekly idea-sharing sessions to post ideas on an idea board. The idea board can be divided into idea stages, making it possible to move the ideas between phases of elaboration, evaluation, selection, testing, and implementation.

You may set monthly challenges in which teams should document or video record their best ideas. You can use push messages regularly on an app to remind everyone to record and write down their new ideas.

There will be some good ideas. Maybe even some great ideas. However, it is worth noting that idea systems will also be full of bad ideas. Lots of the ideas will be based on opinion rather than on true insight. And most ideas will not be based on serious long-term creative efforts.

You need an effective method for evaluation and selection in order to manage all these ideas. If managed well, the idea system can become an important source for continuous innovative activities.

Who can run such an idea system? The committee for evaluating and selecting new ideas will set the direction for future developments. As such, they become key stakeholders in the future survival of the organization. Therefore, you need to ensure that those involved in the evaluation and selection have a good sense for great ideas. They should be knowledgeable and experienced in your work and industry. But they should most certainly be visionaries as well. They should be able to see the potential in ideas that others may reject as nonsense or uncertain.

Reward Structures for Creative Efforts

Was that a smile? Were my leaders positively surprised? Is she trying to give non-verbal feedback expressing how she likes my idea? I hope so!

You like positive feedback on your ideas. This type of feedback helps create motivation to move forward with your ideas. It increases the likelihood that you will speak out about your ideas in the future, making it possible to create a circular effect that brings about more ideas in your organization, eventually building a creative culture.

Internal motivation seems to be the key driver of creative efforts. Are you fascinated about your idea? Are you having fun working on it? Are you curious where it may take you? These questions can help you answer how internally motivated you are about your new ideas.

The higher the internal motivation, the more likely you will succeed with your creative efforts. However, it is complex to set up reward structures that stimulate internal motivation. I will come back to these internal motivation factors later in this book.

It seems that most reward structures tend to stimulate external motivation. Luckily, some types of external motivation can also have a positive impact on your creative efforts.

Rewards can be any type of feedback that stimulates creative thinking and behavior. As such, rewards could include a smile, gift, bonus, or verbal expression: "You are great at what you do!"

It may be recognition of your creative efforts in front of your colleagues: "Let's all give them a hand for their genius work."

It can also be a more permanent recognition like a medal, a diploma, or an "Employee of the Month" award.

One of the best rewards for creative efforts may be encouragement to further engage in the development and implementation of your idea.

The reward does not need to be directed toward yourself. It would be better to direct it toward the actual idea. Imagine if you were to be rewarded a sum of money allocated for you to experiment with your novel idea. To learn more about the idea's potential. Such types of rewards help create a culture where it becomes acceptable to be playful and try out new ideas.

Do you have reward structures in your team? Every social context has reward structures in place. They may be purely informal. They may be based on everyone's personal feedback. Based on everyone's personal beliefs. They may be made up of solely non-verbal and verbal feedback. Are you already highly creative? Then this style of reward structure may work perfectly fine.

Are you not already creative in your team? Then you may find yourself rewarding behavior with negative effects for creativity.

Try recording some of your creativity sessions and decision-making meetings. Now go through these recordings to check how you reward creative efforts.

Try examining all your formal and informal reward structures to check if there are some that may even reward conformity. Maybe some of your reward structures could be updated to stimulate creativity when and where creativity is needed.

Be aware that rewarding creativity can be tricky. **Do you primarily reward ideas that are like your own ideas?** Then you risk creating a culture of conformity toward your own perspectives. Others will eventually strive to present ideas they know you will like. This will reinforce your current perspectives and eventually kill creativity in your team.

Imagine a preschool child making a drawing on a piece of paper. He draws a house, a tree, and a sun. Eventually, a preschool teacher comes by and sees the drawing. The preschool teacher provides verbal feedback to the child. "Wow, what a beautiful house! I love the way you have drawn your tree and sun next to the house."

Next morning, the child starts on a new drawing. What do you think the child will draw this time? Has the verbal feedback made it more likely that the child will draw a house, tree, or sun like the day before?

We like positive feedback. If we figure out what types of ideas lead to positive feedback, it can have a huge impact on the types of ideas we present in the future. This is as close as you can get to the definition of conformity. You will rarely see breakthrough ideas shared in such a culture.

Maybe you should avoid rewarding specific ideas. Maybe you should reward creative behavior specifically: "I love when you help challenge my ideas and perspectives."

You may also reward creative efforts specifically: "Thank you for your time and effort helping me come up with new ideas."

Or maybe you should consider rewarding novelty specifically: "Wow, I love when you bring about new ideas that can take us into completely new directions of thinking."

Nurturing Creative Skills and Confidence

I will now tell you the most provocative thought: It is possible to develop creativity into a habit, so it becomes second nature to you. Yes, you read that correctly—you can nurture your creative potential. It is possible. But it will take practice to become better at creativity. This is true for every skill set in life. It is especially true for creative skills and creative confidence.

When it comes to language, it's not enough to listen to a series of words. You need to practice how to spell the word before it sticks. You need to practice the pronunciation several times before feeling confident using it in conversations. You also need to practice how to use each word in different sentences within different contexts.

It is the same when it comes to creativity. You need to practice creativity in order to develop it into a skill set. You need to practice your individual creative skills and your team's creative skills. The practice must provide successful creative experiences in order to make you confident that you can be creative with any type of problem. Only then can you master your creative potential and be able to engage creatively at will and on command.

There is a serious problem with creative illiteracy. Most people don't know how to be creative at will. Some even believe they cannot be creative. That creativity may be reserved for those working in the creative industries.

Creativity is a fundamental human characteristic. Everyone is creative at a certain level. And everyone can raise this level of creativity. Everyone can become far more creative.

Do you know how to "turn on" your creativity? The good news is that this book can take your creativity to new heights.

Having strong creative skills and high creative confidence will naturally lead to a more creative culture. Creative people produce more alternative ideas. They challenge more complex problems. They will be far more creative during innovative processes and during everyday work tasks. And they will be more successful at evaluating, selecting, and presenting those valuable and novel ideas.

This book is about how you can nurture your and your team's creative skills and confidence. It provides deeper insight into four powerful creative habits. It prepares you for kick-starting your creativity journey to becoming serious innovators.

During the next four sections, you will be introduced to four fundamental creative skills that you can turn into powerful creative habits:

1. Explore new grounds.
2. Imagine novel ideas.
3. Visionary thinking.
4. Persuasive idea presentation.

Ready to develop your creative skills?

Let's get started . . .

HABIT 1

EXPLORE NEW GROUNDS

Challenge what everyone else takes for granted

Beyond Solving Problems

You solve problems all the time during your workday. It is such an integrated part of human nature that you may not even think about it as problem-solving.

When do you put some creative effort into your problem-solving? When you are dissatisfied with your off-the-top-of-your-head ideas? When you are asked for more alternative ideas? When you want to impress others with some novel ideas? If you are curious about whether your next idea may be even better?

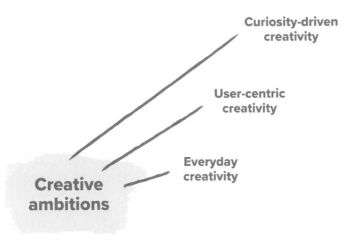

Your ambition determines how much creative effort you put into your problem-solving. It is possible to categorize creative problem-solving into three ambition levels.

The first ambition level is about maintaining current standards. This is typically related to your everyday problems.

The second ambition level is to raise current standards by improving the value you deliver to your users and stakeholders.

The third ambition level is to come up with game-changing breakthrough ideas spurred by your own curiosity.

People who operate healthy, innovative organizations have ambitions at all three levels of innovation. They make sure that their organizations have the necessary creative skills and confidence needed for each ambition level. And they understand how the need for creative skills and confidence may be very different for each ambition level.

Everyone should know how to perform everyday creative problem-solving. However, not everyone may need to help raise current standards. And only a few may need the skills and confidence to produce game-changing breakthrough solutions.

Maintain Standards

The first level is about everyday creative problem-solving. Here, you experience problems. You encounter them right in front of your face. Maybe the machine doesn't work. You experience conflict during your team meetings. Customers complain about product standards. These problems tend to pop up at the worst possibly times, causing stress and needing urgent solutions.

The key to everyday problem-solving is to get back to the standards you used to have. The standards you expect to have. You get back to these standards by solving the problems that appear daily. You must actively search for problems as they appear in order to solve them as quickly as possible.

You may already have some problem-solving methods in place to maintain your standards continuously. If you are in the manufacturing business, you may use LEAN methods for this. You need to integrate creativity into these existing problem-solving methods. Or you may design alternative problem-solving methods using your creativity. That way you will be able to apply creative problem-solving to everyday problems that need better and more innovative solutions.

Everyday problems often need to be handled urgently and with minimum resources. As such, feasibility may be the most important criteria for solutions to everyday creative problem solving.

Raise Standards

The next level of problem-solving is focused on users. It requires a user-centric perspective. Users may be customers. They may be your machine operators, your colleagues, or another department in your organization. It may even be a governmental institution. The user is king for raising standards. It is about going beyond current standards and delivering something better, more efficient, and more useful. You are specifically looking for areas of improvement in your delivery that will provide higher value (or perceived value) for users. Are you actively looking for ways to deliver better value to your users?

Raising standards is driven by the external motivation to meet the needs and pains of your users. You don't always know what makes users happy. Sometimes users will complain to you about a particular problem, but not always. Sometimes they just complain to their friends and colleagues, leaving you in the dark. They may not even be aware of all their needs and pains.

You will need to develop a strong sense of your users' pains and needs; getting into the shoes of your users. You can do role-playing, observation, and interviews. You can spend an extended period of time experiencing what it's like to be your user. Experience your deliverable as the user receives it. You can also invite users into your innovative processes to ensure that their perspectives are represented in your final solutions. As such, raising standards typically has a longer time horizon than maintaining standards. User-centric problem-solving is often organized as a project that takes more than just a few days.

Be aware that no user will ever be able to tell you the *right* pain or need. No group of users will ever represent all users. Even if you were somehow able to engage with all your users over a longer period, you would still not be able to fully understand all their pains and needs.

Your users are not just yours. They live complex lives where they are users of hundreds of products and services every day. They do not have time to reflect on all their user experiences all the time. Most people do not think about their pains and needs related to, for example, cheese packaging, door handle designs, and supermarket payment methods. They may have an opinion about whether a specific cheese packaging works or which cheese packaging is annoying. But they rarely make rigorous deeper reflections on what is the most important problem related to their cheese-packaging-user experience.

You will need to help your users in this process of reflection. You will need to help them see new potential and challenge their immediate understanding of their user experience. You need to study their responses and actions. This will give you a chance to raise the standards of what you deliver to these users.

Users are not just your source of insight. They are also your compass. They make up the key criteria for evaluating and selecting what ideas to pursue. As such, desirability becomes the most important criterion for solutions for user-centric problem solving.

They become the external motivation that helps you navigate your creative efforts. You can always ask the user: Is this what you need? Is this want you want? You are on the hunt for external acceptance of your new ideas. And it feels so good to get positive feedback from your users once you get the idea right!

Set New Standards

At the highest ambition level, you'll find curiosity-driven problem-solving. Here, it's not about problems appearing during your everyday work. It's not about user needs and pains. Rather, it's about what *you* find important. What *you* believe needs improvement. The problems and ideas that motivate *you*. What *you* find interesting.

At this level, you have an ambition to set new standards, to replace existing standards in your organization or industry. These new standards may be related to products and services, production, leadership, delivery, conflict resolution, customer care, communication, or any other part of your organization.

It's about coming up with breakthrough solutions that create a completely new type of value or efficiency. Solutions that have the potential to redefine an entire industry.

If you put all your creative effort into everyday problem-solving, you may eventually end up having the most effective solution fit for the last generation in your industry. Like a superior typewriter that cannot match a modern computer.

If you put all your creative efforts into current user-needs and pains, you will end up having the same solutions as everyone else in your industry. Your competitors are also trying to raise their standards based on the same pains and needs. As such, competitive advantages from raising standards are primarily based on your speed of innovation. Are your competitors uncomfortably close to your standards? Maybe they'll pass you next month.

You need a new starting point for your creative efforts. A high-innovation potential problem to solve. One that is not already taken by your competitors. It cannot be based on your users' pains and needs. It cannot be based on your urgent everyday problems. The new starting point must come from yourself. Your curiosity should drive the creative effort needed for setting new standards.

Curiosity-driven problem solving is based on internal motivation. It is based on your need for personal satisfaction. It is fueled by your urge to make important positive changes in the world. To create something meaningful at work and generally in life. To have fun. To place your mark on history. However, your curiosity can also be based on a feeling that the entire team or industry may be wrong about a certain matter.

This causes you to persevere in the face of resistance. And you will need this perseverance. You may experience resistance from colleagues and leaders. Resistance from other departments, stakeholders, or regulatory institutions. Resistance may even come from customers and users.

Resistance is a natural reaction to novel ideas. Novel ideas often include logic from unrelated industries or new technologies. Some of them may defy current logic in your organization and industry. This is normal for novel ideas. Novelty can easily create misunderstandings. As your audience will not immediately understand the potential of your novel ideas, they may be critical. What they don't clearly understand, they will fear. They will resist the idea until they feel comfortable about its potential.

You are the source of inspiration. Therefore, you will fully understand the problem. You clearly see how current solutions are not fit for this problem. That you need a breakthrough solution to solve the problem. The problem may not be obvious to everyone else right now. But your internal motivation will keep you two steps ahead of anyone trying to interfere with your creative efforts.

Your internal motivation will ensure that critical feedback will not turn into roadblocks. Rather, they will become building blocks for moving forward, making the idea better, and getting it implemented. In other words—your creative efforts will never turn into a simple administrative project. Instead, it will turn into passion and dedication.

To set new standards, you will need to end up with feasible, desirable, and novel ideas. Ideas that can lead to breakthrough solutions. However, during your curiosity-driven work, you will need to use originality as the key criteria for decision-making. You should allow yourself to make decisions based on your own insights. Otherwise, your curiosity risks fading away, eventually killing your creative efforts from within.

Want to set new standards in your organization and industry? You will need strong explorative skills. You will need to challenge what everyone else takes for granted.

You also need an investment perspective for innovation. Think about maintaining standards as a necessary investment for problem-solving. They provide short-term returns, keeping you afloat in rocky waters.

Now, think about raising standards as safe bets. Their strong focus on value will create continuous improvements, leading to increasing returns. Although, in highly innovative industries, you will need to consider raising standards as a bare minimum investment in order to survive in the long term.

Finally, think about setting new standards as an opportunity investment. Its strong focus on novelty creates potential for breakthrough solutions. The kind of solutions that lead to highly innovative opportunities. Creativity is always a chance process. You cannot be completely certain where it will take you. But you can be sure that it will help you keep moving forward.

What are you ambitions for innovation?

Do you have serious ambitions for maintaining current standards? For raising these standards? Do you also have ambitions for setting new standards?

Challenge Standards

I once worked with a zoological garden. I told them to find an interesting starting point for our creative efforts. A problem that most other zoos would never even consider. They came back with an interesting starting point—to challenge the zoo cart deposit system.

You know them from supermarkets. Supermarkets would like you to use their shopping carts because they make it easier to carry and buy more grocery items. However, some users may also use the cart to bring their groceries home, sometimes forgetting to bring the cart back to the supermarket. Other users may leave the shopping cart in the open parking area where the wind catches them, causing scratches to nearby cars. To avoid these misuses, some supermarkets charge a small deposit for each cart. That way they can ensure that users bring back the shopping carts.

You may need to insert a coin in a lock to release the cart. You get your coin back when you return the cart and lock it up. Amusement parks often charge the deposit at a service desk before you are given the cart. Again, you get the deposit back when you return the cart.

Back to the zoological garden. They didn't fear users stealing their carts. The deposit system had been put in place to motivate users to return the carts instead of leaving them at random places in the zoo. But they didn't like the deposit system. They thought the deposit did not match the hoped-for-experience at their zoo. There were no functional problems with the deposit systems. The users didn't find it a problem either. All other zoos and amusement parks nearby had similar deposit systems. Yet, for this zoo, it was still important to find another way. So, we took up the challenge.

The challenge was given to a cross-industrial and cross-disciplinary creativity task force.

One of the task force members worked in the transport planning industry. At the time, his company installed GPS systems in buses to track their location and provide users with expected times of arrival. He suggested putting GPS trackers into the carts. Another suggested installing speakers in the carts. A communication expert suggested connecting the speaker and the GPS so that the speaker could provide geolocation-specific information to cart users and other guests nearby.

When the cart was near the lions, a story about the world of the lions would be told from the speakers. When the cart drove by the ice cream store, a story about the delicious homemade ice cream would be told.

All the way through the zoo, users would be told interesting and childlike stories about all the animals, the playground, the history of the zoo, and everything else. Childlike, because the users of carts are mostly families with children. Each story would have tracks of various length, so it would be possible to hear the end of each story, no matter how slowly or quickly you walked between the attractions at the zoo.

The final story track would not finish until the cart was returned to the service desk. The children would want to hear the end of the story, right? And they would complain to their parents if they left the cart in the middle of the park. They wouldn't want to miss out on the end of a story. A sign on the cart would say: "The story will end when you return the cart." The hope was for cart users to be motivated to return the cart so their children could hear the end of the story.

With this new system, we would no longer need a deposit. A new motivation had been introduced. A motivation based on new experiences for the users, in particular the children. A motivation for the parents to return the cart without money being involved. We challenged a standard that everyone else takes for granted—the zoo cart deposit system. We came up with a potential alternative solution for this standard. A solution that may be valuable in a lot of other zoological gardens and amusements parks around the world. And a solution that brings new value to the zoo experience. New values that were not even directly related to the zoo cart deposit system.

Disposable Coffee Cups

Challenging standards is an effective procedure for identifying new and motivating starting points for your creative efforts. Starting points that have a higher potential for innovative solutions. It's the simplicity of this procedure that makes it so powerful. Everybody can apply it to any kind of problem area.

Let me give you an example. Imagine you're trying to rethink a disposable coffee cup. A one-time-use coffee cup. And you want to have a good starting point with the potential to lead you to some innovative ideas. Now think about what is standard about a disposable coffee cup. What is never really challenged? What does everyone in this industry take for granted about disposable coffee cups?

Most disposable coffee cups are cylinder shaped. Let's challenge that. You challenge it, not because there are obvious problems that need to be solved. Not because there are complaints from users about the shape. You challenge it simply because it seems it has never been challenged before. There may be some potential about the shape that no one else has ever thought about.

Maybe you can design a disposable coffee cup like a bowl, like you normally see for wine glasses. Maybe you can give it a stem to wrap your fingers around, a bit like a lollipop. It could all be designed as a paper construction. Now you can hold it like a lollipop as you walk around with your disposable coffee cup. This will prevent you from having to hold your hands around the hottest part of the cup. And when you take a sip, you can hold it like a wine glass. More elegant and with a better grip.

From this new starting point, you get into an interesting direction of thinking. It may need further development. And maybe the idea will never work. You must remember that creativity is always a chance process. Most ideas will never be used. It's worth exploring whether there's something unique, something valuable, or something interesting about this new direction of thinking regarding disposable coffee cups. Maybe some of its new elements can change the way you understand a disposable coffee cup. Or maybe these new elements will produce some completely new uses. And sometimes, you will be rewarded with a brilliant breakthrough solution.

Let's try another challenge. Most disposable coffee cups have a flat lid with a mouthpiece designed for the shape of the mouth. Let's challenge that.

Imagine the beer bottle design. The neck of the beer bottle is typically wider at the lower part and narrower at the top part from which you drink. The top is completely round. Imagine if the lids for disposable coffee cups were designed the same way. A lid to be used on standard disposable coffee cups. A lid that shapes into a small round top from which you can drink. How would it change the experience of drinking from a disposable coffee cup? How would it change the experience of walking with your cup? Maybe you would spill less on your shirt while walking with your disposable coffee cup. What benefits do you see in this new type of lid?

Let's try a third challenge. Most disposable coffee cups have an open design structure where the entire cup of coffee is filled into one container. Let's challenge that.

What if the cup had inside layers? Maybe these layers will separate the coffee into two or more compartments. Maybe in the bottom compartment it is possibility to keep the coffee warm for longer. Maybe it's possible to insulate the bottom compartment better than the top compartment. The top will cool more quickly, making it possible to drink a few minutes after brewing. Once you have drunk the top part, you can open the bottom part, allowing you to drink warm coffee for longer.

Let's go a bit further in this direction of thinking. Imagine a disposable coffee cup consisting of several detached compartments. Like coffee "Lego" bricks. You put together two bricks if you want a small coffee. You put together five bricks if you want a bigger coffee. Need coffee for the entire office? Bring a bag of coffee bricks and your colleagues can choose for themselves how many bricks they put together. Maybe some bricks contain milk or syrup. Click them together and they will crack open, connecting the coffee compartments into one "real" disposable coffee cup. Can you see some benefits from this new direction of thinking about disposable coffee cups?

Challenging standards can quickly help you get into new directions of thinking for your problem areas. It helps you look for interesting starting points for your creative efforts. Starting points that you would not normally notice in a standard problem definition process.

Challenge Common Sense

Common sense is your way of working turned into standards, norms, and traditions. You need to challenge common sense in your team to find more effective, innovative, and valuable ideas for your future ways of working.

Challenging common sense is hard. You go against the grain; against the common logic and recognized causality in your team. Therefore, you will meet lots of resistance. Challenging how you organize yourselves is far more complex than challenging a product, a machine, or a website design. The way you work and your relationships with others is a tricky area of creativity. It easily becomes very personal. There is a fine line between *you* as a person and the way *you work*. If the way *you work* is challenged, you may mistakenly feel that *you* are the problem.

Challenge is never an attack on any specific person or any group of persons. It is never personal. You challenge to explore if current notions in your common sense need new perspectives. As such, challenge is a healthy way to check if you somehow got onto a bad development track. Maybe everything seems to work fine. But maybe, just maybe, you are blinded by your norms and traditions. Go check if you can do things differently, better, more effectively, and with greater value. Maybe you can even cut out some of your working processes completely.

What do you take for granted? What things have "always been done this way"? What things seem impossible to be do differently? Let's challenge these.

It may be the way you make decisions. Maybe most of your decisions are made during meetings. Could it be done differently?

Your team may communicate internally, primarily using emails. What if you banned internal emails?

Challenging common sense can seem provocative. And it's not something you should do every single day. Rather, think about it as a continuous procedure that should be integrated into your weekly, monthly, or annual creative efforts.

Mapping Standards

You may start by mapping your standards. Go through your work processes, machine handling, meetings, communications, products, and services, as well as customer interactions, websites, and other types of relations. Go through your daily tasks. Map everything that everyone seems to take for granted.

By their very nature, standards are hard to identify. You will not immediately notice them. You need to explore your work moment by moment to see clearly what your standards are. Use outsiders to help identify standards in your team—visitors, friends, suppliers, or customers.

Or maybe you get a new employee or an intern. Allow your new employee to spend the first week looking for standards in your team. What thinking and behaviors are standard and never challenged? Allow your intern to do a project searching for standards. The novice mind of an intern makes it easy to see patterns that you will never notice yourself.

You can also record your meetings. Record your everyday work tasks, operations, and interactions. Analyze the recordings to look for standards and common assumptions in your team.

Now, it's time to challenge some of those standards. You may have identified five standards. Or you may have as many as fifty standards to challenge. Start off by challenging those standards that you are 90% certain cannot be changed. Next, go on to challenge those standards that you are 80% certain cannot be changed. And so forth.

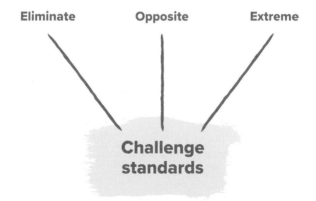

But how do you challenge a standard? Well, if you are highly creative, it comes quite naturally. However, you may need some structure to support your challenge procedures. Try to go opposite, go extreme, or go eliminate.

Go Opposite

What if you do the opposite? *Go opposite* is a structured approach for challenging standards. It can help you develop specific directions of thinking to understand your problem area better. To see if a particular standard may have potential to become an innovative starting point for your creative efforts.

Imagine challenging standards related to a bus. What is standard about a bus? First, there are seating areas. That's standard in most public busses. Second, you enter from the side of the bus. Third, the bus has windows. And often these windows are placed all the way around the bus. There may be more standards related to a bus.

Let's pick a standard to challenge: seating areas. Now you go opposite on the seating areas. What if it was the opposite way? What if it was backwards? What if it was in reverse order? What if it was upside down? What if it started at the end? What if it was turned around? These are different concepts of going opposite in relation to seating areas.

How may *reverse order* affect the seating area? In most busses you enter the bus and then you take a seat. Now imagine a bus where you take a seat before entering the bus. What would that be like? It may be that the seats for physically impaired users can rotate inside and outside of the bus. Free seats may rotate to the outside of the bus as the doors open, making it easier for physically impaired users to take a seat. As the bus doors are closing, the seats rotate back to the inside of the bus.

What if the seating area was designed the *opposite way*? In most busses, you sit up straight. Imagine a bus designed for you to lie down. Maybe it could be designed like bunkbeds with two or more layers. Or maybe the opposite way would mean being physically active.

Give it a go for yourself—try challenging standards related to a bus. See what happens when you go opposite. Be playful. Be explorative. Don't reject a direction of thought because it sounds weird. Think about the weirdness as a steppingstone for new insight. As a step into the unknown. As an opportunity to understand the problem area from a new perspective.

Go Eliminate

What if you get rid of it? *Go eliminate* is another structured approach for challenging standards.

Let's eliminate some of the standards related to a supermarket. In most supermarkets, grocery items are displayed on shelves. Supermarkets often have shopping carts and baskets. They also have strong lights so you can see all the grocery items clearly.

What happens if you simply remove one of these standards? Would the supermarket still work? Could it function in an interesting new way? Or would you have to substitute it with something else? Maybe it can be substituted with a new kind of component, material, place, interaction, technology, motion, shape, or meaning?

What if you remove the strong light in the supermarket? Maybe this will make shopping more of a cozy experience. A café-like feeling. It may create a more relaxed and enjoyable shopping experience in the supermarket.

Will it be more difficult to find the grocery items you are looking for? Sometimes, it may be nice to have a strong light so you can see the grocery items on the shelves clearly. Maybe the shopping carts and baskets could light up in front of you? Maybe it would be possible to turn these lights on and off. Could this save energy? Maybe these new lighting baskets and carts can also be part of creating a completely new shopping experience in a supermarket.

Let's eliminate another standard in a supermarket: grocery items being presented on shelves. What if you removed these shelves? Maybe you could redesign the packaging of grocery items. Ask suppliers to redesign the packaging so the grocery items can be stacked easily and safely. Stacked into pyramids, towers, and mountains.

Maybe the grocery items could hang directly on the walls in the supermarket. The supermarket would need to be redesigned with far more interior walls to create a labyrinth feeling when going shopping. These walls may be flexible, making it possible to move the "grocery walls" in order to put the weekly sales items in focus. This will create new weekly supermarket labyrinth routes for the customers.

Maybe the grocery items can hang in baskets from the ceiling. So, you pull down a basket to take your grocery items. And back up the basket goes when you let go. The basket could hang at different heights. So some baskets hang closer to the floor, others a bit higher, and so forth. It will become a new type of supermarket: a basket supermarket.

You could also create a vending machine supermarket. Imagine a supermarket with hundreds of vending machines. Each vending machine may have ten to forty different grocery items inside. One vending machine may offer cheese. Another may offer milk. Yet another may offer sausages. Go to the relevant vending machines. Pick your grocery items and swipe your membership card. Out comes the grocery items you want. Your payment will be debited directly from your bank account.

Try it for yourself—try eliminating other standards in a supermarket. Maybe you can start by eliminating the shopping carts?

Go Extreme

What if you do far more or far less? *Go extreme* is a third structured approach for challenging standards. It can help you identify new starting points for creative efforts. New starting points that you may never have considered.

Let's go extreme with standards related to a restaurant. There are a lot of different types of restaurants with completely different standards, including all-you-can-eat restaurants, take-out restaurants, and drive-through restaurants. It may be easier if you go for a particular type of restaurant: an à la carte restaurant. Such restaurants are typically organized around tables. You read through the menu while sitting at your table. A waiter will take your order at your table. Taking the order is typically performed in two steps. First, you order a main meal and maybe an appetizer. Later, you may order a dessert or coffee. Other standards in such restaurants include your food being served at the table and having the food served on plates.

What happens if you go extreme on these standards? Make far more or far less of something? Far more time? Far more frequency and length of interactions? Far less object volume, strength, or size? Far more ingredients? Far less duration?

What if the plates were much higher? Each plate could be a table in and of itself.

Dinner for two? Connect your two plates so it creates a table for two.

Table for four? Connect four plates.

Maybe this can enable a more flexible and dynamic table setup. Maybe you will no longer have the problem of two guests occupying a table for four. At first, the restaurant is a wide-open space with chairs. No tables. As food is served the tables are formed. When you finish your food, the table is taken away. This will make it easier to sit close to your family and friends. It will also make it easier to create space for a dance floor as customers finish their meal.

What if you significantly increase the number of interactions with the waiter? What if all customers were given a walkie-talkie or a messaging device to communicate with the waiter? Maybe the waiter can be outsourced to a call center far away.

Need water? Press the water illustration.

Want four customized sandwiches? Press that "talk" button on the walkie-talkie to provide details.

No need to wait for the waiter. Order as you decide what you want. Maybe this will increase sales. Maybe it will make the ordering system more effective. Maybe it will be more fun for kids to order.

Can you see other potentials for the plate tables or the instant-waiter service? Try it for yourself—try exploring some other extremes related to a restaurant.

Ridiculous Starting Points

Go eliminate, go extreme, and *go opposite* will take you in directions of thinking that are often absurd, weird, strange, and ridiculous. That's a good thing!

It's okay to go through this process and end up with mostly strange ideas. Creativity is a chance process. You will not end up using most of the ideas for anything. But the process itself gives you the opportunity that maybe you will identify some interesting starting points that ignite more successful creative efforts. You just need one good starting point to get started. Just one good problem.

Do you dare to challenge your standards?

Problem Exploration

Where to invest your creative efforts? In a standard search for high potential problems, you often end up having only a few alternative opportunities.

Sometimes you may need to go beyond these limited opportunities. To see your problems from new perspectives. And to get a wider range of interesting problems from which to choose.

Creativity is a scarce resource. Creative efforts take up time and energy. You cannot be highly creative with all problems, all the time, all day, and all week. You need to direct creativity toward the problems that are most meaningful and have high innovative potential. **You need to invest your creative efforts into the most promising problems.**

Think of problem understanding as a creative activity. You need to explore alternative problem definitions to understand the problem area better. Each new problem definition gives you a new perspective. The problem exploration will help reveal new understandings that you may never have considered.

Let's take an example. Imagine your problem area is about bruised bananas in your supermarket. You don't want bruised bananas since they eventually develop black spots. Few people like these black spots on bananas. You want to solve this problem. But what is the problem really about?

Your immediate understanding of the problem may be that users handle the bananas incorrectly. Supermarket customers may touch several bananas before they pick the ones they want. Some customers may put them at the bottom of the shopping cart, eventually placing heavier grocery items on top of the bananas. Other customers may store their bananas incorrectly at their home before eating them.

Are you confident that this is the most promising problem? If you are highly confident in your first understanding of a problem, then you should be concerned. Confidence in immediate problem understanding should always trigger an alarm bell. You may be right. Maybe most bananas get bruised because of the customers' handling them incorrectly. And maybe the "It's always the customer that does it wrong" perspective could be a good starting point for your creative efforts.

But maybe you are wrong. Maybe you are limited by your patterns of thinking. Limited by some previous experience in the problem area.

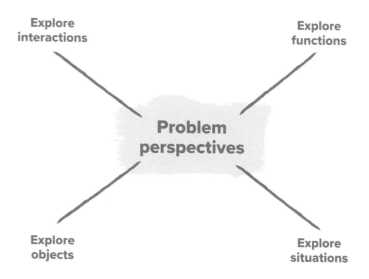

You may need to explore more perspectives related to your problem area. Explore all functions related to the problem area. Explore all interactions related to the problem area. Explore all situations related to the problem area. Explore all objects related to the problem area.

Start off by exploring specific *situations* related to the problem area. For example, the banana space in the supermarket.

Customers may touch several bananas before they pick the ones they want. What may be the different ways customers touch the bananas? And what may be the reasons why they touch so many bananas? They may grip the tops of the bananas in order to get a 360-degree view of the state of the bananas. They may squeeze it in the middle in order to feel the softness of the banana. They may move some bananas around to get to those below. They may touch the bananas because of bad eyesight. Kids may touch them out of curiosity. And eventually, the customers may grab the bananas when putting them into their shopping cart.

There may be more ways and reasons for customers to touch the bananas in the banana space in the supermarket. Use your imagination. You may also use observation, interviews, and experiments in order to explore this problem area further.

Let's explore a different situation: the handling of the bananas at the checkout situation.

The bananas are placed on the belt. Customers may put them next to or up against other grocery items. They may even put them under other grocery items. Some may keep them away from the belt, giving them to the checkout staff only when they are about to be scanned. The checkout staff will also handle the bananas. They may put the bananas on a scale or hold them in front of the scanner. The checkout staff may put the bananas on another belt leading to the bagging area. Other grocery items may squeeze the bananas as they arrive at the end of the belt. Customers put the bananas in a bag or a cardboard box as they leave the supermarket.

Other situations to explore may include the handling of the bananas in and around the customer's car or bike, the handling of the bananas during the walk from the supermarket to the customer's home, and the handling of the bananas when unpacking at home. Each of these situations need to be explored.

You can also try to look at the *objects* related to the problem area. You can look at the banana peel as an object. Is it strong enough? Does it clearly warn about the fragile structure of the banana?

The shopping bag is another object. Are shopping bags designed to protect fragile grocery items like vegetables and fruits?

Shopping carts and baskets are also objects related to the problem area. Where and how do customers place their bananas in the cart and the baskets? Give it a try yourself—try exploring one of these objects related to the problem area.

Now try exploring all the other functions, interactions, situations, and objects related to the bananas in the supermarket.

Ideas as Problem Exploration

I once worked with a company from the beverage infrastructure industry. They make cooling systems, tubes, dispensers, handles, and taps for beer in bars. They wanted to challenge the beer container. The beer keg. So we needed to explore the problem area related to a beer keg. Quickly, an idea emerged about making a beer keg out of paper.

What were we supposed to do with this idea? Ignore it? Can such ideas be helpful as part of a problem exploration? Yes, surely, they can!

What are the building blocks for ideas? Knowledge and experience! So, the paper keg idea is based on knowledge and experience related to beer kegs. You may once have used a traditional beer keg. Maybe you have observed how the staff in a bar handled a beer keg that needed to be changed. You may have seen a movie or documentary involving a beer keg. Or you may have a friend with a bar in the basement.

This paper keg idea can help you gain access to some of your knowledge and experience related to a beer keg. And this will help give you a better understanding of problems related to the beer keg.

You may remember some recent experiences related to a traditional beer keg. Maybe you went to a bar last week. They changed the beer keg while you were waiting at the bar. You saw how the empty beer keg was difficult to handle. It seemed inconvenient to lift. You saw how it was difficult for the staff to find a good spot to place the empty beer keg. You heard them talk about how it may be stolen if they placed it outside at the back of the bar.

You may easily have identified all these problems without much effort. However, some experiences are more difficult to remember. Some you gained later that night as you got drunk. Other experiences with the beer keg may go back thirty years. How do you get access to this type of experience and knowledge related to beer kegs?

Let's get back to the paper keg idea. First, this idea can be a problem in and of itself. Turn any idea around and you will have a problem. The idea is to make a paper keg. The problem is *how* to make a paper keg. Hereby, you get a circular understanding about ideas and problems. Creativity is a constant movement from problems to new ideas, from ideas to new problems, and so forth.

More importantly, the idea itself offers some insight for better understanding the general problem area related to traditional beer kegs.

The paper keg idea suggests that traditional beer kegs are heavy. That they do not fit into standard public garbage containers. That they must be transported back to the beer producer for cleaning and refill. That they will not easily fit on the back of a donkey for transport in rural areas (like paper would adjust to the shape of the donkey). That they do not have an easily printable surface (like paper). It is difficult to place logos and seasonal prints on the traditional keg like the name of the bar or "Happy New Year" illustrations.

The paper keg idea makes it easier to identify these types of insights. Insights that come from your own knowledge and experience. Insights that may not have been so easy to identify without the paper keg idea. Try identifying more problem insights about traditional beer kegs from the paper keg idea.

Most people like to separate problem exploration from idea production. To think of these as two separate steps. That the problem comes first, triggering the other. And yes, you should avoid spreading your creative efforts into all kinds of problems.

It is worth considering problem exploration as the prior step that tells you which problems to invest your creativity into. However, during your problem exploration, you should welcome any ideas that pop up. Use them as steppingstones to explore more perspectives related to your problem area.

There is another good thing about using ideas as part of your problem exploration. Ideas are personal. Ideas do not just come from any knowledge and experience. They come from *your* knowledge and *your* experience. They are based on your personal insights. They often represent what you find most important related to the problem area. As such, your ideas can help make your problem exploration more personal. You will end up with more internally motivating problems. Personalizing your problem understanding has a positive effect on your engagement during your creative efforts. It also increases the likelihood of a more novel output.

Well-Defined Problems

Try to produce some ideas for solving the following problem: How can you make the world a better place?

At first, you may find this problem easy. Now, look at your ideas. Are they practical ideas? Most likely not.

If the problem is ill-defined, you will tend to produce ill-defined ideas as well. Your ideas may be something like: "We need to be nicer to each other. We should be more environmentally friendly. We should help those in need." These are not practical ideas. None of them are actionable. They are not even real ideas. They are more like titles for idea groups.

You need well-defined problems for your creativity to take off. This is particularly true if you invite other people into your creative efforts. Everyone will have to understand the problem and the purpose of their creative work clearly. It is hard to be creative about problems you don't understand. The more well-defined the problem, the easier it is to understand.

Let's take an example. Imagine you want to make your meetings more effective. This is a relatively ill-defined problem. Your ideas may be something like: "Make the meetings more interesting. Make them more focused. Make them more inclusive." What is really meant by each of these ideas? If you were asked to implement these ideas, what would you do?

You need to change this ill-defined problem into one or more well-defined problems. Think about them as sub-problems. You split up the ill-defined problem into several well-defined sub-problems. They are more focused. They are better for your creative efforts.

How to organize the first five minutes of a meeting to make it more effective? Now, *that's* a well-defined sub-problem!

How can you organize an effective distribution of responsibilities toward the end of your meetings? How can you avoid distractions during your meetings? How can you redecorate your meeting rooms, so they support effective meetings better? These are a few other well-defined sub-problems.

Let's take another example: imagine you work at a hotel. How can you improve the user experience for visitors to your hotel? This is a very ill-defined problem. You need to divide it into some well-defined sub-problems.

How to improve the experience visiting the hotel lobby? This is still a bit ill-defined. How to improve the experience of picking up your key at the hotel lobby? Now, this is a well-defined sub-problem. This will kick off your creativity.

How to improve the hotel room experience? Again, this is an ill-defined problem. How to improve the experience of going to bed in the hotel room? Much better. Now it is well-defined.

Here is a trick for turning ill-defined problems into well-defined problems: turn the ill-defined problem into several well-defined interactions, objects, situations, and functions.

Take a few minutes to identify some well-defined sub-problems related to room reservations, hotel rooms, checking out, and hotel cleaning.

Did you find some interesting well-defined subproblems?

Now, pick the most interesting well-defined sub-problem and think up some ideas for it.

Do not merge these sub-problems into one less well-defined problem. Keep them separate during your idea production. Think of them as separate problems you are tackling.

Maybe you will find some ideas that solve all your sub-problems. And maybe you won't. But keeping them apart during your idea production will help you produce more actionable ideas. And more novel and valuable ideas.

Problem Sources

Do you find it hard to get started on problem exploration? There are some key problem sources that may help you gain a deeper and wider understanding about your problem area.

Talk to your users. Talk to your customers. Present your problem to colleagues from other departments or other companies. Listen carefully to what they say. Go observe the problem area. Observe and talk to everyone involved in the problem area. Everyone including cleaners, operators, salespeople, leaders, and public regulators. Try to put some children into the problem area to get their uninhibited fresh perspectives. Talk to experts, researchers, and competitors. Talk to retired personnel from your industry. All of these are valuable sources to involve as part of your problem exploration.

The first source should always be yourself. And your team. You need to empty your own mind first. Get all your understandings and perspectives on paper. Other people's perspectives are good, but they can easily create strong patterns in your thinking. Subsequently, you may end up getting stuck in their perspectives and be unable to see your own perspectives. They could end up blocking your own understanding of the problem area.

Imagine you want to improve customer service in your real estate agency. Think up all your perspectives related to this problem area. Empty your mind. Challenge what everyone else takes for granted. Explore as many problems as possible. Turn ill-defined problems into well-defined sub-problems. Now what?

Set all your perspectives and problem understandings aside. You have them on paper. You can always get back to them later. But for now, you need them set aside. You need an explorative mindset searching for perspectives and problem understandings that you have not yet thought of. Find some domain experts. This could be researchers or professionals with years of experience related to the problem area. Domain experts are often highly reflective in terms of the problem area. They tend to be explorative themselves. Therefore, they are a perfect companion to your problem exploration.

Imagine your problem area is related to effective meetings. Domain experts do research on effective meetings. Domain experts have years of experience facilitating effective meetings. Involve such domain experts to help you explore this problem area.

Now go talk to, observe, and engage with your users as well as other people directly involved in the problem area. These are the participants in your meetings: colleagues, external partners, suppliers, and customers. It may also include cleaning personnel. And those who buy interior elements for your meeting rooms. It could also include participants in meetings from other companies and other contexts.

Observe what is happening during the meetings. Step outside. Take a "fly on the wall" perspective. Join the meetings. Interview the participants before, during, and after the meetings. Record the meetings and analyze the recording. Make random reflection stops during the meetings. Get as many different perspectives as possible for potential problems related to effective meetings.

Are you ambitious about innovative solutions? Involve even more sources into the problem exploration. Involve laypeople into your exploration. It may be hard to imagine laypeople for effective meetings. Everyone has been in a meeting. And most have experienced either effective meetings, ineffective meetings, or both. But maybe you can identify some people or organizations who rarely have meetings. Get them involved in your problem exploration.

Do you need to involve all these sources? No. The smaller the problem, the fewer sources. The bigger the problem, the more sources. The more ambitious you are about innovation, the more sources you will need.

The Real Problem

You have now finished your problem exploration. Imagine having twenty-eight interesting problems to choose from. Now, you just need to identify which one of them is *the real* problem. The root problem. The problem that will solve all other problems related to your problem area. The true problem that will take you to the one and only perfect solution. Wait! What? Is there really such a thing as a real problem for creativity? The answer is yes. And the answer is no. It all depends on the type of problem area.

Problem exploration is a bit like planning an adventurous trip. Bad problem exploration will take you to the wrong destination. You may get to an interesting place; maybe even a better place than what you were hoping for, but it is not the place you wanted to go. Some like this type of completely unpredictable traveling, but most like to know the full budget before embarking on new ventures. You, too, may like to reduce risk, increase efficiency, plan which type of problems you invest in.

Putting a lot of creative efforts into unexplored problems may lead you to interesting ideas. Valuable ideas. Novel ideas. And you may choose to implement some of these ideas to solve some of your other problems. However, most organizations need structure and project management. If you choose to be creative about office chairs, then you want new ideas about office chairs. You are not interested in ideas about dog shelters or kindergarten safety measures. So, in most creative efforts, you need a rigorous problem exploration. You need to identify relevant, motivating, and interesting potential problems for your creative investments. Yet, how will you identify the real problem?

You need to distinguish between two types of problems: complicated problems and complex problems.

Complicated problems can be explored by analysis. Analysis is often considered as the gold standard for understanding complicated problems. Imagine constructing a high-tech adventure house. You may need thousands of electrical, internet, and security wires installed in the walls, floors, and ceiling. One day, your computer system gets hacked, and you lose all the descriptions, drawings, and the overview of how these wires were placed and connected.

To solve this problem, you need rigorous analysis. Eventually, the analysis will lead you to the solution: new descriptions, drawings, and overview.

A complicated problem does not need much creativity. It needs analysis and a catalog of historical solutions as inspiration. This catalog may include previous solutions from your team, your organization, and industry. For complicated problems, it makes sense to identify the real problem. The better the analysis, the closer you get to the real problem. And the closer you get to the real problem, the easier it is to identify the perfect solution from your list of previous solutions.

Now, imagine a different type of problem. Imagine you want to examine potential new uses of mobile speakers in elite soccer practices. Or imagine you want to invent a completely new approach for performing job interviews to find more suitable leaders for your teams. These problems are not *complicated*. They are *complex* problems.

Complex problems include a degree of uncertainty. You may never have experienced this problem before. Circumstances change so your catalogue of previous solutions can no longer help solve the problem satisfactorily. You have higher demands than previous solutions can deliver. Your list of previous solutions is outdated. You are in uncharted waters.

Analysis uses the past to predict the future. Analysis cannot give you the full picture if you want change. If circumstances are changing or new technologies are pushing the industry into a new direction, analysis can still be useful. However, analysis alone will be far too weak for understanding complex problems.

Analysis may help you understand part of a complex problem. But you need something far more human to understand these types of problems better: You need creative insight. You need to imagine and visualize potential future scenarios to form a better understanding of your complex problems. This requires creative efforts. As such, you need a circular experimental attitude toward complex problem-solving. You do not have enough data to point toward what the real problem is. Instead, you need to select problems based on your qualified hunches.

Which problems "smell" most promising? Which problems can help you learn more about the problem area quickly? You need to make a series of bets to get started; to see what ideas you produce for these problems.

Once you get a new insightful idea, you will suddenly see the problem area from a completely new perspective. The idea will help you redefine your complex problem. Eventually, it will give you a more qualified hunch for selecting the next well-defined sub-problems for your creative efforts. Take a second round of creative efforts for these new problems. This will continue until you get a novel, valuable, and implementable solution for your complex problem.

Once you start implementing your final idea, you may get yet another new insight. Suddenly, you will understand the problem area even better. You can now take another round of creative effort based on this new problem understanding. It's a never-ending story, working on complex problems. Luckily, creativity is fun, motivating, and rewarding in and of itself. Once you have gained creative confidence, you will come to love this never-ending circle of creative efforts.

Let's go back to your adventurous trip. Want to go where others have already been? Those who came before have probably made a map. They have made it possible to plot the destination into your navigator and get a direct route. They may even have made a lot of suggestions for how to get there with low risk and high efficiency.

Want to go where most others have not yet been? Prepare yourself for going into the unknown. There will be no navigators and no suggestions of how to get there. You may get there faster than you could ever have imagined. However, you may need some creative effort on the way. No matter what, prepare yourself for a bumpy road.

Problem exploration is a deliberate and continuous change of perspective on the problem area. As such, problem exploration gives you a better foundation for deciding what problem to solve. It gives you a good starting point for your creative efforts. However, at times you will only understand the problem once you get an insightful new idea. Try to backtrack your new insightful idea to see what key problem is solved related to the problem area. In hindsight, you will see the idea redefine the problem for you.

Problem exploration is essential for creativity, but sometimes you need to consider creativity as a dynamic activity where problem exploration leads to creative efforts, which lead to better problem exploration, again leading you to a new round of creative efforts. And so forth.

Problem Boundaries

Is your problem area within the boundaries of your influence? Exploring problem boundaries is a reality check.

Will you be able to implement potential solutions for your problem area? You need to check these boundaries. Can you take action if you get a really good idea for this problem area? You need to check for real boundaries. However, you need to be cautious about your cognitive boundaries. Don't be limited by your cognitive boundaries, but let the real boundaries help you direct your creative efforts.

Constant hesitation can kill your creative efforts. Is this the right problem to be working on? Do none of your ideas seem implementable? Are you trying to solve someone else's problem?

It can feel meaningless to produce ideas that lie outside your boundaries of influence. A boundary check will give you assurance about the seriousness of the problem during your creative efforts.

Imagine you're trying to rethink a coffee machine. And you're specifically trying to rethink the water refill for kitchen coffee machines. A well-defined sub-problem could be: "New ideas for how to refill the water tank."

Let's check boundaries for this problem. Do you have influence over the design of the water tank? Yes. You can now produce ideas for redesigning the water tank.

Let's push the boundary check a bit. Do you have influence over potential connections to nearby water supplies? Like a water tap, pipe, or tube?

Do you have influence over where users place their coffee machine? How close they place it to an existing water supply? Yes. You can now produce ideas for connecting the water tank to an external water supply.

Let's push the boundary a little bit more. Do you have influence over the design of the water supply? The design of the water tap, tube, or pipe? Can you influence the water tap designer? No. Then you should not produce ideas for redefining the water tap to fit your water tank connection.

Let's take this in another direction. Do you have influence over the type of water supply available for users?

Do you have influence over users buying water refill tanks, bottles, or pads to put into the coffee machine? Coffee is mostly water. So, maybe it would be possible to sell exclusive water pads for coffee machines; pads with perfect water for making coffee. Water pads with soft water, pads that extend the life for the coffee machine, pads that make the coffee taste better. Do you have this kind of influence? Yes. You can now produce ideas for alternative types of water supply.

Checking the boundaries of a problem area is a creative activity. You explore potential limitations for each problem perspective. You qualify your potential starting point for your creative efforts.

Four-Step Problem Understanding

Do you need structure for your problem exploration?

Exploration can be a natural part of your daily habits. You may do some exploration on Monday mornings on your way to work. Later, you may explore some potential areas of improvement with a colleague over a cup of coffee. Later in the evening, while taking a long bath, your mind starts challenging a fundamental notion in your team. Something that is not right. Something that needs to change. You don't know the solution yet, but your mind cannot let it go; it keeps exploring.

Build your exploration skills. Develop an explorer's confidence. This way, it becomes part of your way of working. Like second nature—you won't need to plan, structure, or facilitate exploration. It will be part of your everyday work and general life.

Sometimes, you may need structure. Your team may not have gained the confidence or skills to explore well. And sometimes, you work with creative illiterates. Now you need to structure your explorative procedures.

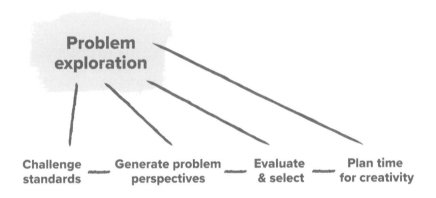

Problem exploration

Challenge standards ___ **Generate problem perspectives** ___ **Evaluate & select** ___ **Plan time for creativity**

It is possible to structure exploration into a four-step problem-understanding tool. Use this tool for developing better problem understanding before you begin important creative efforts. Use it to challenge your immediate problem understandings. Use it to identify problems with high innovation potential to work on.

Step one

Identify assumptions, traditions, and fundamental understandings related to the problem area. What does everyone take for granted? Challenge those standards. Go eliminate? Go extreme? Go opposite? Be playful. Perform an open-ended exploration. It's not about quickly identifying a "perfect" problem definition. It's far more important to identify what has not yet been challenged. What are the limitations in the way you currently think about the problem area? Break out of these limitations.

Step two

Write down as many problem definitions as possible. Generate as many problem perspectives as possible. Turn each ill-defined problem into several well-defined sub-problems. Break down ill-defined problems into situations, functions, interactions, and objects. Observe, engage, and involve users, experts, colleagues, and others in this step. Get as many different perspectives on the problem as possible. Others may have understood the problem area in a way that you have never considered.

Step three

Go through all the different problem definitions and understandings developed in steps one and two. Evaluate and select the most motivating, interesting, and highest innovation potential problems.

In most cases, it is not possible to use analysis to identify the real problem that needs to be solved. For complex problems, you will often only know which problem is the right one once you have solved it; once you have tried it out; once you see its effect during an experiment.

You will need to select a problem that seems promising and feels right; a problem that, once solved, can lead to important new learning. Evaluate interesting problem definitions against all the other problem definitions you have produced.

It's fine to identify and select more than one. You can have two, three, four, or five problems that you are working at the same time throughout your creative efforts.

Check the problem boundaries before starting up your creative efforts. Are your problems within your level of influence? Will you have the power to implement potential solutions for these problems?

Creativity is a chance process. You may get to the breakthrough solution. However, sometimes you won't. It might not be possible to identify a motivating, interesting, and high innovation potential problem. Maybe you need to repeat steps one and two to get more alternative problems from which to choose.

Step four

You have challenged current standards related to the problem area. You have generated a large amount of alternative problem definitions and perspectives. And you have selected what you believe to be the most important problems to solve.

Now you need to reserve time in your calendar for your creative efforts. Reserve time for being creative yourself. Reserve time to be creative with others like team members, customers, users, and stakeholders. Make sure they also set aside time in own their calendars to be creative with you. Creativity requires dedicated effort. You need to reserve several rounds of dedicated time for creativity; on your own and with others.

Set aside specific dates and specific times where you can be undisturbed and uninterrupted. Not just physically, but also mentally. Do you have other important decisions to be made on the same day? Then move your creative efforts to another day. Stress, big decisions, and other important matters can easily diminish your creative efforts. Urgent matters tend to win over creative efforts in your daily work.

HABIT 2

IMAGINE NOVEL IDEAS

Dive into your ocean of new opportunities

Beyond Viable Solutions

Do you want to produce new ideas that ignite innovative activities? To come up with better ideas related to your work processes, products, services, sales, leadership, or any other problem inside and outside your organization? All organizations need a constant flow of new ideas to challenge declining ideas.

Do you know how to produce novel and valuable ideas at will? Are you confident that you can produce such ideas whenever asked to do so? Can you do it individually? Can you do it with your team? Can you do it right now?

Most have relatively low creative perseverance. Therefore, you often end up with only a few ideas to choose from. And it is rare that any of these ideas are novel.

Imagine working on a project. You need a new idea; a new solution for a problem in the project. You start thinking, one idea pops up. Does it work? No, not really. Another idea pops up. Will this one work? No. A third and a fourth idea pop up. They still don't solve the problem. Now a fifth idea pops up. This fifth idea seems to work.

You start to like this idea. It's much better than the previous four ideas. And it really seems to solve the problem. Deep down you know there may be better solutions. But right now, you have an idea that will work. You settle for this idea and stop your creative efforts.

This is a perfect attitude for standard problem-solving. You produce ideas until you have a viable solution. Any further creative effort is a waste of time.

Let's agree that standard problem-solving has little do to with perseverant creative efforts. During creative efforts, you are not satisfied with a viable solution. You go for better ideas. You go for novel ideas. You go for valuable ideas. You go for ideas that make the problem go away for good. You go for ideas that you have never considered. You go for the "Why haven't we thought about this before?" type of ideas.

You need far more creative perseverance for this. You need an imaginative mind. An imaginative attitude that does not settle for viable solutions. An attitude toward creativity that the next idea may be much better than the previous ones. An attitude to want more ideas from which to choose. Because it gives you a better foundation for decision-making.

You need creative skills to imagine novel and valuable ideas. You need to develop creative confidence to produce ideas at will and on command. Now producing new ideas will be easy, serious, and fun.

Pattern Thinking

Do you find it difficult to come up with novel ideas? Coming up with those surprising ideas that inspire yourself, colleagues, and leaders? Why is it so difficult to produce those ideas? Well, it is partly because of your patterns of thinking.

Your knowledge directs your patterns of thinking. Your previous experiences make the patterns stronger. And your regular routines create fortifications around these patterns, making it hard to come up with novel ideas.

These patterns are helpful in your everyday life. They make sure you can easily retrieve memories of previous viable solutions. Viable solutions to solve the problems you face daily. The patterns help you make quick decisions when navigating through everyday situations.

About to cross a busy street? You don't need novel ideas for such a situation. Crossing a street is a standard problem. Rules on how to cross a street do not suddenly change. Circumstances are stable and "street crossers" rarely have innovative ambitions finding new ways to cross the street. Therefore, you can trust your previous viable solutions for how to cross the street in front of you.

Living in a big city, you will hardly think about how to cross a busy street. You have developed a strong pattern for such situations because you cross busy streets all the time. It's such a strong pattern that your thinking most likely happens subconsciously. You can easily cross the street while having a conversation on the phone, drinking a cup of coffee, all while greeting other pedestrians.

Patterns make life so much easier. Except when you need to be creative.

Patterns direct your thinking in familiar directions. That is why simple brainstorming sessions typically end up with some standard ideas you have already thought or heard of.

The patterns direct your thinking to previous viable solutions for similar problems. You don't need previous viable solutions when you are trying to be creative. You want new ideas. New solutions. You want to diverge from these previous solutions and go in completely new directions of thinking that can take you to novel and valuable ideas.

Are most days alike? What about your morning routines? Do you get up around the same time? In the same way? Eat the same thing for breakfast? Read the same newspapers? Same route to work? Same type of chatting with colleagues as you arrive at work?

What about your evenings and weekends? Do you go to the same sport weekly? Do you meet with the same friends and family regularly? Have similar conversations about similar topics? Are most days alike?

Are most of your routines the same every day? Yes. Then don't expect novel ideas to suddenly pop up in your mind daily.

You can still be creative. But you may need to structure your creativity. Stimulate your creativity whenever you need to be creative. And practice your creative skills.

Patterns can also be created in a very short amount of time. In teams, patterns can be created in a matter of minutes. Imagine working in a team of four. You are trying to solve a problem. You have agreed to use brainstorming to come up with some ideas.

None of you had thought about the problem prior to the brainstorming session, except for Eric. Eric had an idea for how to solve the problem. He got the idea before your brainstorming session. He got the idea last night. And he has been thinking about the idea several times up until your brainstorming session. In fact, Eric has come to like his idea quite a lot.

Eric decides to present his idea immediately as your brainstorming session starts. And what a presentation. He presents the idea very persuasively to the other team members. Now think about this situation. How do you think Eric's idea presentation will affect the remaining part of the brainstorming session?

Eric's idea creates a strong pattern of thinking for the entire team. Most likely, Eric's idea will become dominant in everyone's mind. It will become a focal point for your discussions. You will elaborate on this idea. You will come back to this idea several times. And it is likely that you may even end up choosing this idea as your final solution for your problem.

Ideas presented in the early phases of a creativity session can end up as a mental fixation for the team. The same is the case for examples. Examples of how another team solved a similar problem. Or an example of how you solved the problem last year. These examples create patterns that are hard to break.

There will always be a "first" idea to be shared in a brainstorming session. That's how a brainstorming session works. You think up and share your ideas with the team. These first ideas can create strong patterns. Patterns that you need to get around if you want to move in other directions of thinking, coming up with more ideas, coming up with very different kinds of ideas.

Reflect on how your workday may be affected by strong patterns of thinking. Do your meetings often start with a powerful presentation of one idea? Does this "first" idea sometimes become dominant during such meetings? Do you end up choosing this "first" idea as your final solution?

Maybe you need structure to go beyond these strong patterns. Maybe you need the creative skills to think up new ideas that diverge from such dominant ideas. Maybe you need the creative confidence to imagine novel ideas for any problem and in any situation. Your creative confidence is often what makes the difference between just being able to do it and actually doing it.

Novelty High

Let's do a short creativity task. The task is to rethink work processes related to a supermarket checkout situation. Imagine a busy day in the supermarket. There are long lines of customers waiting to get to the checkout to pay for their groceries. There are a lot of problems you can solve. Customers may find it difficult to self-organize in straight lines. It all seems a bit chaotic. There are loud noises. Some customers are slow at putting their groceries on the belt. Could the scanning of the groceries be done more efficiently? The payment. How can that be done in a different way? Putting the groceries into bags and carrying them home. Could that be done in a more effective way? You may find other more interesting well-defined sub-problems related to the supermarket checkout situation.

Try coming up with new ideas for one or more of these problems related to a supermarket checkout situation. As many different ideas as possible. As novel ideas as possible. Please spend about ten minutes producing ideas for this task. Try to focus only on your production of ideas. Shut down your computer, phone, and tablet. Don't use the internet. Don't ask colleagues or friends for help. Do your best being creative on your own. Good luck.

Let's reflect on your creative performance during this task. The first thing you look at is quantity. How many ideas did you produce during the ten minutes? First, remove all duplicates. What's left is your total production of ideas. Don't think of this number as a universal indicator for your creative performance. It is not a real test in any way. Rather, think of it as a short experiment on how many ideas you can produce in ten minutes.

Did you manage to produce around ten ideas? That's a fine production of ideas. Did you produce more than twenty ideas? That's perfect. You're good at producing a large number of ideas in a short period of time.

Next, reflect on the quality of your ideas. Quality is about the level of novelty. It is also about value. For this short individual reflection, you should use "surprising" and "inspiring" as indicators for the quality of your ideas.

Did you produce an idea that somehow surprised you? Were you surprised when you came up with it? Surprised because it offered a completely new way to look at the supermarket checkout situation? Did you produce an idea that is new to you? That somehow inspired you with a new element or a new solution? An idea that you haven't seen used in a supermarket checkout situation?

If you are unsure, then try presenting the idea to a friend. Was your friend surprised or inspired by the idea? If yes, then you have gotten yourself a point for quality. Remember, this is just a short creative experiment. We will go much deeper into the evaluation of new ideas in a later chapter. Now, check if you came up with more of these surprising ideas.

It's a good idea to reflect on your ideas from a more social perspective as well. How surprising and inspiring are your ideas compared to ideas produced by other people? Let's look at some ideas produced by other people.

Imagine replacing the belt with a vacuum-like scanning machine. You no longer put your grocery items on the belt. Instead, you place the vacuum-like machine onto your shopping cart or shopping basket. The vacuum-like machine will gently suck the grocery items through a scanning-tube. Out come the groceries on the other side. You are now ready to pay.

This idea is distinct from current solutions in most supermarkets. It completely rethinks how your groceries are handled and scanned at checkout. Try comparing your ideas with this idea. Are your ideas more inspiring? More surprising? Are your ideas more novel?

Imagine a completely different idea for a supermarket checkout situation. The idea is to replace the entire supermarket interior with a running-sushi-restaurant-like setup.

Want to shop? Find a table. Enjoy a coffee while all the supermarket grocery items are displayed on a moving belt running by all the tables, including your table. You don't need to move around. The groceries come to you. Pick the grocery items you want directly from the belt. Just take them. Put them into the basket next to your table.

Done shopping? Ask a waiter for a bill for the coffee and all your groceries. This idea rethinks the entire shopping experience. Try comparing your ideas with this idea.

These two idea examples may help you get a feeling about the quality of your ideas.

Do you want to know how to produce more novel ideas?

Let's get right into it . . .

Idea Combinations

I once worked with a commercialization unit focused on research-based inventions. We were looking for new business opportunities for some of their unused patents.

One of these patents uses electro-magnets to create wheel resistance in gym exercise bikes. The patent idea is to use electro-magnets interacting with the spinning wheel. Increase the power of the magnet to raise the resistance. This will make it harder to push the pedals. Reducing the power will decrease the resistance. This will make it easier to push the pedals.

At that time, the market didn't accept this patented idea. Commercialization wasn't easy.

We put together two teams to look for new market opportunities. The team members were highly diversified, including physicists, engineers, designers, and business and communication people. They worked for 48 hours on developing alternative ideas for new uses of this patent.

How may this patent idea be useful in a pharmacy? How may it be useful in a bus? How could doctors use this patent idea during operations? The teams systematically imagined how the patent idea may create new value across all kinds of objects, professions, and organizations. They came up with hundreds of interesting new uses for the patent idea. They also came up with several weird and crazy new uses that would never work.

Eventually they came across air duct systems. Here they found a feasible, novel, and valuable new way to use the patent idea to significantly reduce the energy consumption related to the air fans.

That's a powerful process for idea production. And yet, it is quite simple. It's all about looking for new combinations across objects, professions, and organizations. Looking for combinations that are meaningful and lead to novel and valuable ideas.

Idea combination is the most powerful procedure for producing new ideas. It is an underlying fundamental procedure for general creativity tool kits. Most creativity tools are based on this simple procedure. Learn how to combine existing ideas in new ways, and you will find it easier to produce novel ideas for just about any type of problem.

Idea combination connects two pieces of knowledge in a new way. Two experiences in a new way. It connects two previously unrelated ideas in a new way. To look for meaning in this new connection. Does it work? Does it provide a new understanding? A new opportunity? A new idea? No. Connect two other ideas in a new way. Does this work? Do you now have a great idea? Yes.

Let's go back to the supermarket checkout situation. We will now rethink the checkout situation using idea combination. Remember some of the problems related to the checkout situation? Making customers wait in line. Putting groceries items onto the belt. Scanning those groceries. The payment situation. Getting the groceries into bags.

The checkout situation represents one piece of knowledge, one part of the experience, one of the ideas for the combination.

We will now identify the other piece of knowledge. Another part of the experience. The other idea to add to the combination. The formula is as follows: supermarket checkout + unrelated idea = potential new idea.

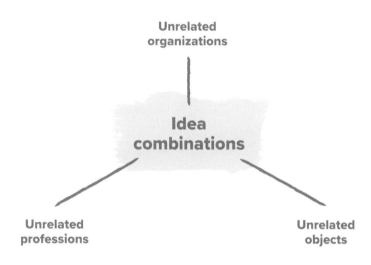

It's hard to identify other existing ideas from out of the blue, but you can look for inspiration in unrelated objects, professions, and organizations. What unrelated organization may have a similar type of problem as seen in the supermarket checkout situation? Similar at a principal level. Similar in the sense that they also have people waiting in line; people may also have to put their stuff on belts, because they also need scanning, or other similarities to the supermarket checkout situation.

Look for interesting features in these unrelated objects, professions, and organizations. Interesting features from which to be inspired. Interesting features to put into your combination. Therefore, the formula can also be as follows: supermarket checkout + interesting unrelated feature = potential new idea.

Let's take an unrelated organization: an airport. Airports are unrelated to the supermarket checkout situation, at least if you ignore the tax-free shops. Can you find some similar problems or interesting features in the airport?

At the gates, users will line up before boarding the airplane. That situation involves similar problems as in the supermarket checkout situation. Airport gates often have chairs for the users to sit in while waiting for their turn to board. Users will be called to the gate when it's their turn to board: users with small children first, then first class, business class, priority users, and so forth. What would happen if you combined this idea with the supermarket checkout situation?

Imagine a supermarket checkout situation with a seating area. You take a number upon arrival at the checkout area. You take a seat. You will be called to the next available checkout station when it's your turn. Maybe the system can prioritize elderly people or customers with children. Maybe you can even leave your shopping cart or basket when you take your number. That way, all your groceries are scanned, and you are ready to pay once you are called to the checkout station. Supermarket checkout + airport gate = supermarket checkout number-and-priority system.

Let's take one more. Can you find another problem in the airport similar to the supermarket checkout situation?

At the airport security check, users put their hand luggage onto a belt. That situation involves similar problems to the supermarket checkout situation. Does this situation offer an interesting feature from which to be inspired? Plastic boxes. Users put their hand luggage and jackets into plastic boxes. The plastic boxes are put on the belt and takes the hand luggage through a scanner. What would happen if you combined this idea with the supermarket checkout situation?

Imagine the boxes being attached to the shopping cart. They replace the current shopping cart basket. Maybe it is possible to hang two or three detachable boxes on the cart. As you shop, you put your groceries directly into the boxes. You put fruit and vegetables in the top basket. You put water, wine, and other heavy stuff in the lower basket. And you put bread and cereals in the middle basket. That way, the bananas will not get squashed by heavier groceries during shopping.

Arriving at the checkout station, you detach the boxes from the cart. You put the boxes directly onto the belt. No need to pick up each grocery item individually. You now only need to do a maximum of three actions to get all your groceries from the cart onto the belt. And your groceries lie safely in the boxes as they move along the belt. No squeezing or pushing against other grocery items. Supermarket checkout + airport security check = detachable boxes on shopping carts.

Let's take a third combination for the supermarket checkout situation. And let's forget about the airport. The bakery profession may have some similar problems. Bakers wait for their bread to bake in the oven. But do they stand in front of the oven waiting? No. They use a timer to alert them when it's time to check on the bread. What would happen if you combined this interesting feature with the supermarket checkout situation?

Imagine the shopping cart handles having a "checkout" button with a timer attached. You press the button when it's about time to go to checkout. This will take you into a digital line. Now the timer gives you an estimated waiting time before it's your turn at a checkout station.

Thirty seconds? Then you go directly to the checkout station indicated on the timer display.

Six minutes? You don't need to wait in line. You can spend your six minutes checking the "newly arrived grocery section" that is conveniently placed near the checkout stations. This may increase sales and provide a more relaxed checkout experience. The timer will alert you when it's time to go toward the checkout station. Supermarket checkout + baker profession = checkout alert timer on shopping cart handles.

Now we have some ideas for the supermarket checkout situation. We got the ideas using idea combinations involving the bakery profession, the airport security check, and the airport gates.

It's about identifying unrelated objects, professions, and organizations to look for similar problems and interesting features for inspiration. To see what happens if you make the combination. Does it create new meaning? Does it lead to new ideas? Maybe a novel idea? Maybe even a valuable idea? Remember that creativity is a chance process. You will develop a lot of useless ideas. But you may develop the insightful breakthrough solution for your problem.

New Connections

The ideas must be previously unconnected. Idea combinations will only work if there is a degree of unrelatedness; a high degree of newness for the new connections. Otherwise, they don't lead to novel ideas. The connections should at least be new to you.

Imagine the following idea combination: supermarket checkout situation + another supermarket checkout situation. How is this going to lead you to novel ideas? Maybe the one supermarket has been doing some creative thinking, finding new solutions. The other supermarket can imitate these new solutions in their supermarket. This is not really what is meant by making new connections.

It can be super effective to do imitation. Every supermarket should consider imitating competitors when they come up with good ideas, but you won't be the creative one. And the procedure itself is not creative at all. Creativity comes when you make new connections yourself.

Your friend may come up with a great setup for her home office. A setup that makes it far easier, more effective, and enjoyable to work from home. If you imitate her setup, you may get a great setup yourself. Your friend was creative; you conformed to her idea.

Direct imitation does not lead to novel ideas. You use direct imitation to catch up with your peers.

Creativity sees new connections. Connections that have not been established before. Idea combination requires a transformation of ideas from unrelated domains to fit into your domain. That's the heart of idea production. This will take you beyond your peers, coming up with better ideas and inspiring your peers to follow your ideas; making them want to imitate you.

Imagine the following idea combination: pen + marker. These objects are not identical. But they are quite close. It is likely that they have been used as inspiration for each other several times before. Therefore, this combination might not lead to any novel ideas.

Markers are often thicker than pens. What if pens were thicker? Maybe this will make them more attractive for advertising purposes. Some companies put their logo or name on their pens and give them to potential customers as part of their advertising. Maybe thicker pens could have more than just a logo and a name? Maybe it would be possible to print catchphrases, illustrations, or even highlight this month's discount on such thicker pens? Pen + marker = advertisement pen.

Give this a try yourself. Try finding other interesting features from a marker to improve a pen. It's not an easy task!

Imagine the following idea combination: pen + thermostat. At first, this may seem like a strange connection. However, it's likely that this combination may never have been used before. To you, it might also be a new connection. Let's try it out.

A thermostat regulates temperature. It activates a heating or cooling device when the temperature reaches a certain point: too cold or too hot. What if a pen could regulate temperature?

Construction workers may get shaky hands during the cold winter months. This makes it difficult to read their notes, drawings, and figures. What if a pen can produce heat during cold winter months? It will heat the hands of the construction worker. Maybe that could stop the shaking hands. Such a pen may make communication on construction sites more effective during winter.

The activation of heat could also have a different trigger. Have you ever tried making notes upwards while lying in a sofa chair or a bed? Gravity pulls back the ink, so the roller ball dries out. Or maybe you have been writing in a room without gravity? Not likely, but anyway. Without gravity, the ink is not pulled toward the roller ball. The pen stops putting ink on your paper.

What if the heat activation could be triggered by the angle of the pen? When the pen points downward or sideways, it will not activate heat. However, when the pen points upward, it will activate heat while the roller ball is "in use." The heat will affect a heat-expandable material inside the pen. This material will push the ink toward the roller ball, and it will be possible to use a roller ball pen upside down. Pen + thermostat = anti-gravity pen.

Let's try a completely different kind of connection. Clothing store + furniture store. At first, this combination may seem a bit boring. Will it really lead to a novel idea? Let's see what happens.

Most furniture stores design themed showrooms. These showrooms make it easier for customers to visualize how the furniture may look in their own homes. Large furniture stores may create several themed showrooms for girls' bedrooms. Maybe there is a red showroom with minimalistic children's furniture and a yellow showroom with wooden furniture. Maybe one showroom for girls aged three and six, and another for girls aged seven to ten, and so on.

Interested in a new desk chair for your girl's bedroom? Bring it to the showroom that is most like your girl's bedroom. Now you can get a better feeling of how this furniture will work for you. Furniture stores have themed showrooms for bedrooms, kitchens, bathrooms, and living rooms. Even showrooms for different kinds of terraces. They create showrooms for the most common uses of their furniture.

What if you introduced themed showrooms in a clothing store? The showrooms should make it easier for customers to visualize how the clothes would look in their own environments: at home, work, school, and sport; or even at a wedding, nightclub, bar, or restaurant. Large clothing stores could have several showrooms.

Want to try out some new swimwear? Go to the beach showroom. Here you will find the floors colored like sand. There will be a sun bed for you, and you will have very strong light. Look in the mirrors on the walls. How do you look in this swimwear in a beach setting?

Want to try out some office clothes? Go to the meeting showroom. Here you will find a large office table and office chairs. Have a seat. Look in the mirrors on the walls. How do you look in these office clothes in a meeting setting?

Want to try out some clothes for going out? Go to the restaurant showroom. Or the bar showroom. Here you will find bar stools and a dance floor. The light will be dimmed. And you can turn on the disco ball. Look in the mirrors on the walls. How do you look in these clothes while dancing? How do you look when sitting on a bar stool? Look in the angled mirror on the ceiling. What do you look like from above the first floor in a nightclub?

Give it a go for yourself—try out some idea combinations and look for meaningful new connections. Spend a few minutes on each of the following exercises. Try to be playful, and be patient with yourself. You don't have to prove your creativity to anyone, not even yourself. This is a "sandbox" environment. And remember, creativity is a chance process. Do not look specifically for breakthrough solutions. Simply try out the new combinations and see what happens. Some ideas will be crazy. Others will be boring. Some may surprise you.

Office chair + balloon = new idea?

Hints for interesting features: balloons can inflate and deflate. They can expand in size. Balloons are fun to play with. They are disposable. Balloons are made of rubber. You can connect balloons using a string. Find other interesting features yourself, and connect one or more of these features with the office chair. Have fun.

Here are some more exercises for you:

Office chair + kitchen pot = new idea?

Office chair + pilot = new idea?

Hotel reception + fast food restaurant = new idea?

Hotel reception + police officer = new idea?

Hairbrush + shower head = new idea?

Hairbrush + dentist = new idea?

Meeting + movie theater = new idea?

Meeting + green screen = new idea?

Hair salon + real estate agent = new idea?

Hair salon + kindergarten = new idea?

Sources of Inspiration

How can you find the right source of inspiration for idea combinations? There are basically two approaches. One approach is to look for similar problems in unrelated objects, professions, and organizations. The other is to take something completely random. Which one is for you?

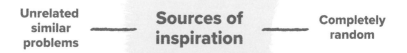

Similar problems from unrelated sources

Looking for similar problems is dependent on your level of understanding of the problem. You will need to understand the problem at a principal level in order to find similar problems across objects, professions, and organizations.

Let's take an example. Imagine you are trying to rethink a shoe. You want to find alternative ways to fasten the shoe. Alternatives to laces, Velcro, and elastic bands. You need to **take the shoe out of the problem understanding. When the shoe is out, you get to the principal problem.** Fasten ~~the shoe~~. Now you can look for anything that can *fasten*.

What in the world can fasten something? Are there any objects that can fasten? Are there any professions that fasten something? Are there any organizations that fasten something? Anything or anyone that can fasten something may have a solution that can inspire you. A solution that is different from the current solution in your industry. A solution that is based on a different kind of logic. A solution that becomes your source of inspiration.

If the two sides of the shoe are held together, the shoe will not fall off. This is another way to define "fasten a shoe". Let's take the shoe out of the problem understanding. Holding the two sides ~~of the shoe~~ together. So, another principal problem is *holding two sides together.*

Across all objects, professions, and organizations: what can hold two sides together? Maybe you get some immediate thoughts off the top of your head: a magnet. A magnet can hold two sides together. Vacuum. Bolts and screws. Tape. Glue. Air pressure. Eventually, you will run out of immediate thoughts.

Now you look at specific objects, professions, and organizations. For example, a dentist. What does the dentist need to hold together? They sometimes need to hold a tube fixed near your mouth. Some dentists use a clamp to fix the tube. Clamps can hold two sides together. The clamp can go into the idea combination: shoe + clamp = new idea for fastening the shoe.

What about a storage company? What do they need to hold together? They use locks to lock doors to the door frames. A lock can hold two sides together. The lock can go into the idea combination: shoe + lock = new idea for fastening the shoe.

See if you can find other objects, professions, and organizations that hold two sides together.

Now it's time to apply these sources of inspiration to your idea combination formula. Let's take: shoe + magnet = new idea for fastening the shoe. What could this idea be about?

Imagine magnets replacing the laces. One magnet on each side of the shoe. Or several smaller magnets. As the left-side magnets get near the right-side magnets, they stick together. This will hold the shoe on your foot like laces and Velcro. Alternatively, the bottom of a pair of open shoes could be magnetic. Put on your matching magnetic socks. Place your feet over your magnetic shoes. Ta-da. The open shoes will stick to your socks. You are now ready to go. You may need to use electro-magnets so you can switch them off with your smartphone. Such shoes may be interesting for people with chronic back pain and for orthopedic hospital sections.

Try it yourself—try making new connections between the shoe and your new sources of inspiration for what can hold two sides together.

Completely random sources

Let's get back to the random sources of inspiration. Random sources have the power to take you to fundamentally new directions of thinking. To directions where no similar problem may exist. And yet, you will often be able to find sources of inspiration to make meaningful new connections. New connections that can lead to novel and valuable ideas.

Randomness ensures that your sources of inspiration will never be limited by your patterns of thinking. They are random. As such, they block your highway thinking. They offer new, unexplored directions. The best part: it is easier to identify random sources of inspiration. You don't need to understand your problem at a principal level. In fact, your problem and your source of inspiration should have no relation whatsoever; not even any relation for the problem.

How do you select a random source of inspiration? Well, you can have a list of random organizations, a list of random objects, and a list of random professions. You can turn it into a poster or a deck of cards. Close your eyes and pick a random source of inspiration.

You may pick "riding instructor". This is your random source of inspiration. What does a riding instructor hold together? The riding instructor needs to hold the saddle on the horse. They use a girth to fasten the saddle around the horse. This is your source of inspiration: a girth. Now put it in the idea combination formula. Shoe + girth = new idea for fastening the shoe.

Your list of random objects may include briefcase, paper clip, mask, freezer, tennis racket, oil tanker, soap dispenser, sauna, whip, purse, necklace, walkie-talkie, axe, and microphone.

Your list of random professions may include tailor, prison guard, carpenter, racecar driver, nurse, photographer, museum director, bus driver, painter, sailor, potter, software developer, diver, rock singer, and car mechanic.

Your list of random organizations may include fire station, university, toy store, television producer, cigarette producer, pharmacy, car manufacturer, pet store, stock exchange, clothing store, tooth paste producer, farm, social media, transport company, movie theater, and airport.

It's preferable that you have primary experience with all the objects, professions, and organizations on your list. If not, then at least have some knowledge about them. It is difficult to be inspired by objects, professions, and organizations you don't fully understand.

Ready for more? You can also add universal innovative principles to your random list. Your list of innovative principles may include vibration, rotation, refill, stacking, magnetism, floating, vacuum, turbulence, sucking, encapsulating, folding, drilling, spraying, segmentation, combining, nesting, counterweight, intermediary, and expansion.

What about new technologies? Yes. Let's also put them on the list. However, given the constant introduction of new technologies, it is difficult to provide an updated list of inspiration. You will have to identify these technologies yourself. And remember to update your list regularly.

There are some interesting types of technologies you can put on your list. Some technologies may have been around for a while. These technologies follow an exponential development curve. They are truly interesting when it comes to creativity.

We have seen how computer processors have followed an exponential development curve for years in terms of performance and price. Other technologies follow a similar pattern, including batteries, IoT and LED. They continuously double their performance or halve their price over a short period of time. This speed of development will constantly create new opportunities across all kinds of industries. As performance increases and prices are lowered, these technologies can eventually enter industries where they have never been valuable before.

Fearless Elaboration

You have now put some effort into producing alternative ideas. You may have thirty ideas. Fifty ideas. Maybe even two hundred alternative ideas for your problem. Some of the ideas are easy to understand. Easy to implement. They are hands-on, and their value is obvious. Other ideas may be less easy to understand. They may seem impossible to implement. And you may be unsure if they will bring about any value at all.

Don't use these immediate impressions to sort your ideas into *good* and *bad*. Some of your ideas will be too premature to be evaluated at this point. You risk using your immediate impression to kill the novel seeds created during your idea combinations.

Think about your ideas from a causal point of view. Which ideas are improvements or add-ons to existing solutions for your problem? Which ideas have a causal relationship with your current way of thinking? Which ideas take point of departure in current logic in your team? All these ideas can be evaluated based on your current logic. You will immediately be able to evaluate these ideas for novelty, feasibility, and desirability. No need to put a lot of effort into elaborating on these types of ideas.

Now, let's look at the non-causal ideas. These ideas are based on logic from a different industry or domain. They may even defy current logic in your team. They are not merely improvements to your current solution. Instead, they offer a fresh new way of looking at your problem. They do not have a causal relationship with your current way of thinking. Therefore, you cannot immediately evaluate such ideas.

Any immediate evaluation risks undermining your creative efforts so far. It will kill the ideas that have potential to lead to novel solutions. The types of ideas that can help you see things differently.

These ideas need elaboration before they can be evaluated or fully understood. They are pre-inventive. They point toward a new direction. But they don't clearly reveal their true value yet.

You need to **dedicate some fearless elaboration to see where these types of ideas can take you.** Fearless because you risk wasting time elaborating on ideas that may end up not being useful. Fearless because you may end up in ridiculous thought experiments. Fearless because you may risk saying something silly. You risk losing face in front of your colleagues, trying to elaborate on the potential of such ideas. Fearless because you may end up with a breakthrough idea.

Fearless elaboration reveals if any of the non-causal types of ideas are more feasible and desirable than the causal type of ideas.

Elaboration is to apply all your knowledge and experience into the further development of ideas; to imagine future scenarios for the idea and to imagine the idea unfolding. What may happen as a result of this idea being implemented?

Elaborating on these ideas can feel like a constant cognitive conflict. Is this a waste of time? This will never work. This is strange. It may feel irrational. At times, it may even feel a bit absurd. You need to tolerate this cognitive discomfort.

The discomfort is a good indicator that you are moving into a new direction of thinking. Do not judge the idea while elaborating. Try to consider these ideas as steppingstones to get to new places. To new ideas. And remember: creativity is a chance process. You are taking a chance on potential novel ideas.

Causal ideas

Let's look at some causal ideas related to the supermarket checkout situation. One causal idea may be to put up more checkout stations. Make the checkout belts longer. Create an alert system for opening more checkout stations when lines get too long. Train checkout staff to handle the scanning and payment more effectively. Buy better scanning equipment. None of these ideas need much fearless elaboration. They are based on current logic in most supermarkets. They are causally related to existing solutions in the supermarket industry.

Non-causal ideas

Now, let's look at some non-causal ideas. One of the non-causal ideas is to replace the shopping cart basket with detachable plastic boxes. The checkout timer button for the shopping cart handles is also a non-causal idea. As well as the supermarket checkout seated number and priority system.

None of these ideas seem to follow current logic in supermarkets. They are disconnected from existing solutions in the supermarket industry. Their logic comes from a different type of organization (airport) and a different type of profession (baker).

Let's look at the supermarket checkout seated number and priority system. The idea is to make it possible for customers to relax in a seating area. To avoid having to stand in line while waiting for their turn at checkout. The ticket system makes this possible.

At first, it may seem like a crazy idea. How do you find space for all these seats? Who should be prioritized? Are the seats necessary? What is the point of this? You don't want people sitting in the supermarket all day. Will customers get into fights about their place in the line when some are seated, and others are standing? Stop! Get out of this cognitive swamp.

The idea offers a new direction of thinking. Take it. Go in this direction, at least for a short while, to see where it can take you. No judgment. Just curiosity. Let's do some fearless exploration.

Imagine the seating area is located outside the checkout stations. Designed with a "cafe atmosphere". Maybe it could be a real cafe in direct connection with the checkout stations. Take a ticket number. Leave your shopping cart. Go find a seat on the other side of the checkout station. Have a coffee, tea, or hot chocolate. The checkout staff will now scan all your groceries. They will bring you your groceries and let you pay at your seat. This is a totally different shopping experience. You will be less exhausted from shopping. You will remember this shopping as a better experience. And you may be more likely to come back to this supermarket some other time.

Let's try an alternative fearless elaboration of the seated number and priority system. Imagine the seats forming the line toward the checkout station. Once you get to the checkout area, you find a seat with space for your shopping cart in front of you. The seat will move forward as the line progresses. The seats are built into the floor like a moving walkway: a moving seating line. This will give you some time to relax before you need to take home your groceries.

Let's try a third alternative fearless elaboration on the seated number and priority system. Imagine that the system prioritizes loyal customers, families with small children, and mobility-impaired customers. You arrive at the checkout area. Find a checkout ticket machine. Scan your membership card. The ticket machine can tell you're a priority based on your membership data. It gives you a ticket number showing your place in the line. This way, supermarkets can offer a fast-track checkout for specific types of customers.

Ready for a final alternative fearless elaboration? Imagine the seats designed around a little play area. That way the seating area can allow for short breaks for families with kids. Do you have a large amount of shopping to do? Take a break halfway. Let your kids play for a bit in the play area. Now you are ready to continue shopping. Other customers may also like a short break in this seating area. Maybe there is a game station or television for those kids that are too old for a play area. Maybe this could be where you put your kids while you continue shopping on your own. Supermarket staff could supervise your kids while you continue shopping.

Fearless exploration is to be curious. It is to ignore the standard judgment. To tolerate the anxious discomfort that comes when you engage with wild ideas. Engage in uncertain ideas. Unpredictable ideas. Imagine what interesting places such wild ideas may take you!

Four-Step Idea Production

You need new ideas in your daily work. You need ideas at unexpected times. Sometimes, you need them urgently. You may need new ideas at eight o'clock in the morning. During a meeting or a difficult negotiation. You need new ideas for what to cook for dinner, what to do for Valentine's Day, for having fun. This unpredictable need for new ideas requires well-developed creative skills and a strong creative confidence.

Yet, sometimes you need to plan your creative efforts. This gives you the opportunity to systematically prepare and perform creativity sessions, meetings, and workshops. To invite relevant people to join the creative efforts. To plan time and space. To prepare creative process steps. It also allows you to prepare for and facilitate those unexperienced in idea production. You need an idea production method to master this planning.

For most people, idea production is a high-cognitive demanding activity. You will need to limit other mental activities in order to direct your attention toward your creative efforts. You need to establish a strong focus to stimulate creativity.

During everyday work, you are often bombarded by the need to be available for all sorts of matters simultaneously. You give attention to colleagues, leaders, customers, and friends. You think about a fight you had in the morning with your kids. You think about what to buy for tonight's dinner. You think about unanswered emails, phone calls, and messages on social media. You think about what the doctor told you last week. And you think about the wedding you are planning for next month. All sorts of thoughts pop into your mind as you try to focus on the problem at hand.

Help your team establish a stronger focus. Find a remote meeting room where others cannot easily disturb your creative efforts. Tell others not to disturb you. Tell them that you are having a serious meeting that requires all your attention. Turn off your mobile phones. Shut down your computers and tablets. Perform a physical or mental exercise to help direct attention toward the problem at hand.

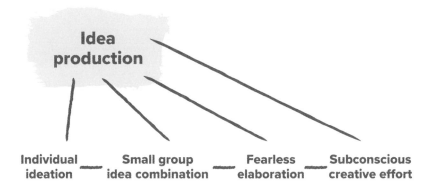

Consider idea production as a four-step method. It will help you produce more ideas. More novel ideas. More diverse ideas. More valuable ideas. More surprising ideas. More inspiring ideas. And more motivating ideas.

Step one

The first step is individual idea production. You take advantage of the probability that each participant comes to the meeting with different patterns of thinking. That each team member is naturally affected by their individual previous experiences, knowledge, and daily routines. Affected by all the other activities leading up to your idea production session.

Participants will instantly go in different directions of thinking as they start their individual idea production. Do not ruin this diversity of thinking by sharing your ideas as they come to your mind. Do not create strong team patterns by allowing ideas to become dominant from the beginning of your creativity session.

One participant may have just finished a meeting prior to your creativity session. One may have seen a documentary last night related to the problem area on a principal level. Another may just have come out of a discussion with a colleague. All participants are primed in different ways as they enter the creativity session. This causes a natural diversity in thinking. Simply allow for individual thinking time. Make sure it is conducted in silence. No one should share their ideas.

Step one may take two minutes. It may take four minutes. Or even ten minutes. If you are highly creative, you may set aside thirty minutes for individual idea production. As the individual idea production slows down, you can continue to step two.

Step one can also be planned based on your total amount of time available for the entire idea production session. If you only have thirty minutes in total, then step one should only be two or three minutes. If you have five hours in total for your idea production, then step one could potentially be much longer.

Step two

This step is a continuation of the idea production. You continue the idea production in smaller groups. Do you have eight participants? Form two to four smaller groups during this step. Do you have fifteen participants? Form five to seven smaller groups.

Smaller groups are more dynamic. They offer a safer space for thinking up and expressing wild ideas. With smaller groups, you avoid creating team-wide patterns of thinking. And the idea production per person tends to be more prolific in smaller groups than what is seen in bigger teams. **Smaller groups help produce more alternative ideas.**

The point of step two is to come up with even more novel and valuable ideas. More than you had during step one. As such, step two is not about sharing the ideas you produced during step one. Rather, it's about getting far more ideas, although the ideas from step one may be involved in the production of new ideas during step two. Step two should provide you with more alternative ideas from which to choose.

Going into smaller groups increases your ability to combine participants' knowledge and experience into new, meaningful combinations; to apply your combined knowledge and experience in order to solve your problem.

Compose your groups to make them as internally diverse as possible. Think about your team as a mental library. The books in your mental library represent experiences and knowledge from your entire life. The books in each group should be as different as possible.

Participants with similar educational backgrounds should go into separate groups. Participants involved in the same sports should go into separate groups. Participants who know each other well should go into separate groups. Divide your team to maximize the diversity of profession, culture, hobby, gender, and interests in each group.

Shuffle the groups every thirty minutes. This will shake up your group patterns. It will mix your knowledge and experience in new ways. If you continuously shuffle the groups, you will increase the likelihood of continuous new connections. As a result, you will get more new ideas. Staying in the same groups for too long risks creating strong group patterns. These patterns can reduce the number of alternative ideas. The patterns even risk turning into strong attitudes that may make your subsequent idea evaluation less open-minded.

During this step, you examine the problem at a principal level to look for related problems from unrelated objects, professions, and organizations. Use them to create new, meaningful connections. Use your list of random sources of inspiration to create interesting idea combinations.

Step two can take anything from five minutes to several days. The more important the problem, the more time you need for this step. Do you have innovative ambitions? Then set aside a serious amount of time for this step.

Step three

While step one and two are mainly focused on quantity, step three focuses on quality. Step three is about elaboration. Going into some of the ideas in depth.

You need to share your ideas with the entire team. To identify ideas that have novel potential. The ideas that may be a bit wild. Those ideas that are different from your current way of thinking; different from your previous solutions for the problem, the type of ideas that offer a new route of opportunities.

You go against the grain. Against current logic in your team. The logic of novel ideas does not easily fit into a team. You need to transform these ideas to make them fit your team logic. Or you need to transform your team logic to better understand these ideas.

You need to be playful while elaborating on these ideas. You need fearless elaboration to transform what seems unfeasible. **Use your imagination to turn what may seem unfeasible into something feasible.** Elaboration can help you see the value in novel ideas. See potential. See more clearly if the novel ideas will work.

Elaborate on all meaningful non-causal ideas before any type of idea evaluation. Elaboration gives the non-causal ideas a chance of proving worthy before being evaluated against the causal ideas.

Step four

Is it finally time to evaluate the ideas? No. Not yet. It's hard to resist the temptation to pick your favorite idea. It will feel natural to share with the others which idea you believe in. To show where you stand. Resist this temptation! Do not share any of your attitudes toward any of the ideas. And do your best to avoid finding yourself a favorite idea. As soon as you pick a favorite idea, your creative thinking will stop.

Step four is about letting your thoughts continue to elaborate on your new ideas. You need to let your subconsciousness continue your creative efforts while you start doing other things. You may go for a walk. Drive home from work. Take a shower. Check your emails. Sort your files. Go for lunch.

During steps one, two, and three, you created a strong creative focus. Allow this focus to continue. Sometimes, you will be rewarded by your subconsciousness. Rewarded with a sudden new insight; with an even better idea, or an idea that connects some of your other ideas in a new way.

Step four is about postponing evaluation until the next day. Next week. Or next month. Picking a favorite idea will end your creative efforts. It will kill your subconscious creative efforts. It will stop your ongoing idea production, and it will focus your elaboration toward just that favorite idea. That's why you postpone evaluation: to get more thinking time before you shut down subconscious creative efforts.

Postpone evaluation until you hit a real deadline. If you don't have to decide before next week, postpone the evaluation until next week. If you don't have to make a decision before next month, postpone the evaluation until then.

If possible, repeat steps one, two, and three several times before you must make your decision. Maybe you have a chance to go through these steps for one hour on Monday, three hours on Wednesday, and forty minutes on

Thursday before eventually having to evaluate and make decisions on Friday. Allow yourself as much creative thinking time as possible. The more thinking time you have, the more likely you will end up with novel and valuable ideas.

Ready to move on?

Next, we will examine how to make visionary evaluations of new ideas.

HABIT 3

VISIONARY THINKING

See potential where others only find trouble

Beyond Standard Evaluation

I once worked with an international medical company. One of their departments had production facilities located in five countries across three continents. They wanted to develop a common language for creativity and develop a corporate culture for applying creativity to make better decisions. They knew they had to think up more alternative perspectives and do some serious creative thinking before making important decisions, continuously challenging their own perceptions. They wanted to listen curiously to other people's ideas, especially when they presented opposing ideas that may conflict with their own perspectives, and visualize potential positives and negatives for alternative ideas. And to do so with a disciplined, open mind.

We designed a twelve-week practice program to exercise these creative skills. To develop it into a confidence and a culture. Every employee and leader went through the twelve weeks of daily creativity practice. We demystified creativity. It became clear when to be creative and how to be creative.

There was a consistent experience of it becoming easier to produce more ideas and ideas of higher novelty. More importantly, we saw increased creative perseverance. People started asking for more alternative ideas before making up their minds. Inviting colleagues to help get around alternative perspectives before getting an attitude for what the best way forward should be. Loosening up the strong positioning that otherwise often occurs during decision-making.

Can I hear your other ideas? The alternative ideas you considered before making up your mind? Before deciding which idea to go for? Before deciding which idea to present today?

A visionary mindset continuously challenges your own perception to widen your perspectives, gain new perspectives, and look for potential where everything seems like trouble. It is to **evaluate new ideas with a disciplined, curious, and open mind**. Ultimately, it is about creating a learning-oriented attitude. To be open toward new ideas, new situations, and new experiences. A visionary evaluation of potential ideas, solutions, and opportunities.

Discussion Favors Old Ideas

You use your intuition to evaluate ideas. You set criteria that help you score ideas, and you discuss. You discuss which idea is best, which idea to select, which idea to test, which idea to implement.

No matter how fine-tuned your intuition, no matter how well-designed your selection criteria, you almost always end up in discussion before making your final decision.

Discussion is a powerful approach for decision-making. A perfect discussion will naturally reveal the best idea. It will make it obvious to everyone what the superior idea is. **However, discussion has one major flaw when it comes to creativity: it favors old ideas**. Discussion favors ideas you know well. Ideas you have seen, heard of, or tried before. It favors ideas with which you have experience.

A standard discussion follows a three-step process. Step one is about positioning. Which idea do you like? Which idea do you believe in? You will each find your position and share your position.

Does everyone like the same idea? If yes, then you may stop the discussion now. If no, then move on to the next step in the discussion: argumentation.

Step two in discussion is to produce and present arguments for your position, for your idea, and against the other positions. The other ideas. Good argumentation will create consensus around one idea. The idea with the best arguments for it. And the least argumentation against it. If argumentation does not lead to this clarity, then discussion can move on to step three.

In this final step, you may use alternative means (alternative to arguments) for convincing the others to come around to your position. To win them over and make them accept your idea. You may even use social or hierarchical powers to win the discussion.

There is a serious issue related to step two in a standard discussion. **It's far easier to produce lots of arguments for ideas you know well** or ideas you have tried out before. It is easier to produce good arguments for ideas you have been using for many years. It's not so easy to produce good arguments and lots of arguments for ideas you just came up with. Ideas you came up with last night or this morning. An overwhelming number of good arguments for a well-known idea can make it difficult to pick the new and less-known ideas. As such, the nature of discussion can end up favoring old ideas over new ideas. Simply because it's easier to produce and present arguments for old ideas.

Arguments are good. Arguments bring perspectives to the surface; new perspectives, more perspectives, more nuances of existing perspectives. However, you need another approach for producing and sharing these perspectives. They should not be used for defending and attacking specific positions or ideas. Rather, they should be used as inspiration. For learning. To help better see each other's perspectives. And to co-create perspectives beyond those in the team. To find perspectives that go beyond what all of you could see at the beginning of the idea evaluation. This leads to the second issue with discussion: early and strong positioning.

Step one of a discussion is about making your position clear. Strong positions can make it difficult to be open-minded and curious about the potential of other positions. Do you believe in your position? Defend it with several elaborate arguments. Attack the other positions. Wait! Maybe there is something interesting about one of the other perspectives. Now how do you suddenly turn around without losing face? Do you risk losing credibility? Will people trust your perspectives in future discussions? Will you lose the discussion?

A culture of strong positioning can kill curiosity. Because it becomes more important to defend your position. More important than trying to understand other positions. You become fixated on your own position. Taking a strong position can lead you into a trap. Make you want to win; make you want to prove that you are right. Make you want to appear rational and consistent.

Evaluating new ideas is never about you. It is not about winning a discussion. It is all about learning. Learn about the alternative ideas being evaluated. Get more perspectives. Get deeper insights into each perspective. Get wider perspectives for each idea. You need to gain insight into each idea before making up your mind or taking a position. You need to postpone positioning until you have looked at all perspectives with a curious, open mind.

Cognitive Flexibility

During idea evaluation, you need the opposite of strong positions. You need cognitive flexibility. A flexibility that will enable you to change your perspective and position several times during the evaluation. To challenge your own perception.

Children are flexible. During childhood, you are open-minded. As a child, you continuously change the way you see things; the way you understand ideas and their potential. And you are curious about new ideas and new situations. What do they have to offer? What can they be used for?

As you go through childhood, adolescence, and adulthood, you gain more experience and knowledge. This makes you less flexible. You find it increasingly difficult to adjust to the new rules of the game, to new technology, to new routines, new regulations, new procedures, new ideas.

You can easily handle ideas that relate to your previous experience and knowledge. Such ideas are easy to evaluate according to what you have seen before. They are easy to understand. Therefore, they create less fear than novel ideas will, less fear than ideas you cannot easily understand, less fear than ideas that you cannot relate to your previous experience.

A less flexible mind can become stubborn. You may invest a lot of time, resources, and effort into defending your perspectives; defending them during heated decision-making meetings, defending them during coffee chats, defending them in front of your friends, this can make it difficult to embrace new ideas that may seem to conflict with your current perspectives;

conflict with your beliefs. You will fear these new ideas. As such, you will tend to favor ideas that follow your previous experience and knowledge.

You cannot trust your current perception when you're evaluating new ideas. You cannot trust it because it is limited to your previous experience and knowledge. You need to think about idea evaluation as a process of challenging your current perception; looking for new perspectives.

To become more visionary, you need to turn on your cognitive flexibility. It will set you free. It will give you a different attitude toward new ideas; a curious attitude. You don't judge the ideas; you don't take strong positions; you don't make decisions before you have understood all possible perspectives and the potential of all ideas suggested.

After a rigorous, open-minded evaluation, you will be able to make up your mind. You may still say no to a new idea, but at least you did your best trying to learn about the new idea before judging it. Maybe a new idea will surprise you. And maybe you end up loving this new idea.

The Woman on the Train

Why are all these perspectives so important? Let's do a short creativity task to unpack this question. It may help you understand better. Understand the meaning of perspectives. What is meant by being a visionary? To envision alternative possibilities; alternative explanations.

Imagine a woman traveling on a train. She's chopping onions. With a kitchen knife. On a cutting board. The other passengers are looking at her like she is a lunatic. What are your thoughts? Why is she on the train chopping onions?

Is she crazy?

Is she a chef? A chef that is late for work preparing the onions for today's menu—onion soup?

Maybe she is an actor going to an audition. An audition where she must act like she is crying. She may keep the chopped onions in her pocket. Ready to use them when she needs some tears rolling down her cheek.

Is she participating in a movie? Some kind of video for commercial purposes? Advertising a new kitchen knife?

Or is she demonstrating the cutting board and kitchen knife to a friend on the train? Perhaps she just bought it at a major discount. And she is trying to convince her friend to go buy one herself before they run out of stock.

Try your best to think up more potential explanations as to why she is chopping onions on the train. Use your curiosity. Try to be open-minded. Find as many alternative perspectives as possible. Envision all possibilities.

Alternative Explanations

Imagine you are presented with an idea you don't immediately understand. You see others handle a situation very differently from the way you would have handled it. Your standard reaction is to judge. Is it good or bad? Do you like or dislike it? Does it seem rational or stupid?

To become more visionary, you need to dig deeper and see the potential in such an idea. See the potential in the alternative approach for handling the situation.

Let's do a few more creativity tasks to examine potential alternative perspectives and understandings before you make up your mind.

Imagine a car parked so it blocks the exit for other cars in the parking lot. Your immediate reaction: "What stupid parking!" No, you should not make an instant judgment. Suspend your judgment. You need to stay open-minded. To look for potential alternative explanations; to look for potential meaningful perspectives.

Maybe the driver of the car received an unexpected phone call while entering the parking lot. A phone call from his pregnant wife. That she needs to go to the hospital. That she is on her way down the stairs toward the parking lot. That she needs help. The driver could not find a free parking space. So, he left the car, and rushed to the nearby building to help his wife back to the car to take her to the hospital.

Or maybe the driver of the car is related to the drivers of the cars being blocked. Maybe they're friends or family. They may leave at the same time later. So, it doesn't matter if these cars are blocked until then.

Maybe the police want the cars blocked. They may have been stolen. It may be that the driver of the car has blocked the other cars to help the police. Maybe the police are on the way right now.

Try it for yourself—can you come up with more alternative explanations for this situation?

Let's try another creativity task. Imagine a colleague working under his desk. Do you find that weird? Try your best to postpone any kind of judgment. Instead, try looking for alternative explanations. Why may your colleague work from under his desk?

Maybe your colleague is trying to watch a video on his computer. The light in the office makes it difficult to see all the details in the video. Your colleague has taken the computer under the desk to get a better look at what's in the video.

Or maybe your colleague is irritated by too many interruptions at his desk. Irritated by all the disturbances from colleagues. In order to focus, he has moved under the desk.

It may also be that your colleague has back pain. That moving under the desk will make it easier to lie down when the pain gets bad.

Or maybe your colleague wants to avoid the draft from the open windows at the office. Sitting under the desk may shield him from the draft.

Try it yourself—try to find more alternative explanations. Good luck!

Disciplining of an Open Mind

Either you have a curious, open mind. Or you don't, right? Well, not really. You can develop a more open mind. You can nurture your curiosity. You can also structure your thinking and interaction. You can navigate toward a more curious open mind during idea evaluations.

It's a matter of disciplining your thinking; disciplining your interaction.

Defer making up your mind about any of the ideas under evaluation. This is a hard discipline. It's tempting to start looking for the best idea. To let your colleagues know which idea you believe is best. It's tempting to make a move, trying to influence your colleagues and affect them with your immediate opinion; to make them believe in the "best" idea too. Don't do it!

Any comments about your position can easily start a traditional discussion. A discussion that favors old ideas. Resist this temptation. Allow everyone, including yourself, to stay open-minded. To look at the ideas without any emotional involvement. To look at the ideas in a more relaxed mode; a mode where you dare look for potential in ideas which may, at first, seem like trouble.

Separate potential positives from potential negatives. They need to be completely separated in time and mind. Do not contrast any positives with negatives. Do not balance any negatives with positives. Do not measure positives and negatives against each other. Separate all thinking and interaction about positives and negatives. Also, do not compare an idea with any other idea. Each idea should be understood on its own. **Each positive perspective and each negative perspective should be understood by itself.**

Take one of your ideas. A random idea. Start off by thinking about potential positive perspectives. What positive consequences may come as a result of this idea if it is implemented? Only positives. Keeping your mind around the positives will create a spiral effect. That'll make it easier to discover even more positive perspectives. A positive perspective functions like a steppingstone for the next positive perspective. Be patient. Allow yourself plenty of time to think. Do not stop thinking just because it is hard. Maybe you can set a timeframe for this. Four minutes. Fifteen minutes. Three hours. Invest plenty of time into idea evaluation if the problem is important.

Next, think up potential negative perspectives. Potential negative consequences that may come if this idea is implemented. Again, create a spiral effect for your thinking. Focus only on negatives.

Imagine a colleague proposing to have one day per week where you're completely offline and completely on your own; no phones, no meetings, no chatting by the coffee machine with colleagues, no computers, no tablets, and not any kind of interaction with colleagues or others. You're on your own. You'll only have paper and a pen. It should help you have dedicated time for focusing on important work tasks. Do you like this idea from your colleague?

You may think it's a strange idea. That it will never work. This will never help you to get all your work done. How can you get things done without your colleagues? Without your computer? Stop! Stay open-minded. Avoid making up your mind. Don't develop an attitude toward this idea. It's not a good idea. It's not a bad idea. Just be curious.

Spend a few minutes thinking up only potential positive perspectives on this idea. How will it positively affect your daily work? Your relationship with your colleagues? Mood? Efficiency? Concentration? Quality of work? Work-life balance? Stress level? Diet? How will it positively affect other things at work and in your general life?

Next, spend a few minutes thinking up only potential negative perspectives on this idea.

Now, spend a few minutes trying to come up with alternative ideas that solve the same problem. Alternative ideas with similar positive perspectives but without the same negatives.

Getting Into the Open Mode

It takes discipline to stick to this structure. Think about it as a disciplining of your thinking, and a disciplining of your interaction. Discipline to not fall back into discussion.

You have grown used to standard discussion. Discussion has become a standard automatic response to any new input, any new idea, any new situation.

You start discussing without even considering when and where discussion is useful. For most, discussion is not a method. It's more like second nature. Therefore, you may sometimes fall back into the standard mode of discussion even when you really want to be curious and open-minded. You'll need to get back into a curious open mindset as soon as possible. Maybe you will need to have a facilitator ensuring the right structure. A facilitator that can help you remain curious and open-minded.

You can perform idea evaluation as a meeting. You can also think about idea evaluation as a series of informal and formal interactions combined with time for individual thinking. The more formal, the easier it is to facilitate the structure.

As you get closer to decision-making, the team atmosphere may change a bit. It becomes more tense. This is a natural effect from discussion, but it can also appear during more open-minded attempts to evaluate new ideas. You need to foster playfulness during idea evaluations; make them more playful.

Playfulness brings about a more relaxed mode, making it easier to stay curious and stay open-minded for longer. Making it easier to play with ideas and perspectives that may seem completely contrary to your previous experience and understanding.

The facilitated playfulness should not make the evaluation less serious. Rather, it should help you to remain serious without falling back into standard discussion. You can be playful without becoming superficial, fluffy, and half-hearted. You can have fun while being completely focused and dedicated.

Prototypes may help get you into a more playful mode. Help each other develop simple prototypes of your ideas. Draw them. Use glue, scissors, paper, and pencils. Developing prototypes will make it easier to share and discover new perspectives together.

Some ideas cannot be prototyped. Instead, such ideas can be turned into role plays. Make up situations where the idea can be played out. A future scenario; a specific situation. Try your best to make it as authentic as possible. Stand up. Walk around. Make a simple stage. Try it out in a real-life context. It can help you discover new perspectives in a playful mode. Do the role play over and over until you get a good understanding of the idea.

A Nose for Good Ideas

You may feel a bit uneasy the first time. Your immediate judgment tells you clearly which idea is best. Why waste all this time considering potential perspectives on all the other ideas? If only you could just tell everyone immediately what was right and wrong, then you could save a lot of time. And you could move on to something more important. But think about it: few things are more important than making good decisions for important problems. A series of bad decisions can ruin any team; ruin the motivation; ruin the future of the team.

Think about it as an investment. You have invested time and effort into identifying an important problem to be solved. You have invested time and effort into coming up with potential ideas to solve this problem. You now need to invest the necessary time to understand all potential ideas before you make your decision. You have planted the seeds. You have helped them grow. It's now time to check their quality.

You may also feel a bit confused. Why should you stay open-minded? What if the others have a hidden agenda or are not open-minded? What if they are not curious about your perspectives? What if they are just pretending or they end up voting for their favorite idea regardless of all the perspectives shared and discovered? Are you the loser then? Because you stayed open-minded?

Loser? A curious, open mind is not about winning. It's about learning. It's about widening your perception. Seeing new perspectives. It's about seeing potential where others only find trouble. It makes you the visionary. The perfect attitude for making important decisions.

But how can you make the final decisions then? You need qualified voters. Not everyone is capable of being curious and open-minded. These visionaries should be prioritized in making the final decision for which idea to go for. Simple majority votes will work for less important problems. **For important problems, you need decision makers with a nose for good ideas.** Decision makers who are good at visualizing idea potential.

You develop a good nose for ideas by listening to new ideas; reflecting on them; playing with them; evaluating them with a curious, open mind; making continuous visionary evaluations for new ideas; making an effort; and reserving dedicated time for presenting, listening, and evaluating new ideas in your team.

Motivate your team to present their new ideas during this time slot. Make sure this time slot is reoccurring. Maybe once a week or once a month.

Create a playful idea evaluation environment. An environment where it's less about finding perfect solutions for urgent problems. Rather, it's about developing a nose for good ideas, and to see if some interesting ideas to implement come up.

The environment should motivate everyone to bring novel ideas. Novel ideas to be evaluated by your team with a curious, open mind. Eventually, this will help develop a nose for good ideas. This will make you all more visionary. This will also help you identify who are the best visionaries in your team. Let them play a bigger role in future decisions regarding your new ideas.

Diversity Included

Consensus creates a feeling of success. You like to reach an agreement as quickly as possible. Therefore, you tend to involve like-minded people in your decision-making processes.

Homogenous teams can make decisions quickly, as they have similar opinions and tastes. They have similar experiences and knowledge. Maybe even similar interests. They understand new ideas from the same perspectives. Therefore, they can quickly reach a unified verdict on new ideas. This is super effective for making quick progress on less important problems.

Sometimes you need to make serious decisions about more important problems. Too often, new ideas are evaluated in homogenous teams, even if the problem is of great significance.

Homogenous teams take less perspectives into consideration. They have a limited understanding of the potential of the new ideas being evaluated. As such, they are less visionary, and they risk rejecting novel and valuable ideas simply because they lack the diversity to discover the true potential hereof.

You can have homogenous project teams, homogenous functional teams, homogenous teams for anything. You may even have homogenous teams working on important problems with high innovation potential, but you must include diversity during your idea evaluations. You may increase diversity by inviting other people into your team temporarily, for example, during a workshop or a series of meetings.

You are not looking for opposition. You don't want rebels coming to your idea evaluations. They risk harming your curious, open mind. Rather, you need to look for people that will contribute with their perspectives without judgment or strong positions. People who can help you discover completely new perspectives. People who can join with a curious, open mind.

You can increase diversity by involving users, lead users, colleagues, customers, stakeholders, domain experts, and others who may relate directly or indirectly to the problem area.

You may also involve idea experts. Idea experts are different from domain experts. They may not be related to your problem area. Maybe they are not even related to your domain. They may have no knowledge about your industry. Rather, their expertise is related to the key logic of the idea under evaluation.

Remember supermarket checkout + airport security check = detachable boxes on shopping carts? An idea expert for this idea may be someone from airport security, or from a company that designs airport security belts and scanners, or from a company that designs the plastic boxes for these belts. An idea expert could also come from a company that produces detachable boxes for any kind of industry—even industries not related to supermarkets or airports.

Idea experts bring their years of experience related to these plastic boxes. They may have seen how users use them in interesting ways, use them incorrectly, or how they reject using them at all. They may have experience about best practices for introducing the boxes to users and personnel. All this experience can help people better understand and evaluate the idea.

Let's take another example of idea experts. Remember the paper beer keg idea? Idea experts for this may not know anything about the beer keg industry. They may not know anything about beer. Rather, idea experts for this idea must know a lot about paper, about paper construction, and about paper packaging for liquids.

Idea experts are good for diversity, because they are often completely detached from the industry logic related to the problem area. They are free to see things differently. And yet, they have deep knowledge related to the idea being evaluated. They can help you see what they see. Help you to see the potential before you make up your mind.

Four-Step Idea Evaluation

Want to facilitate a curious, open-minded idea evaluation? Let's put the structure into a four-step idea evaluation method.

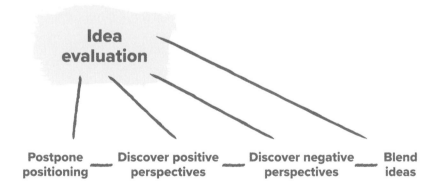

Step one

Postpone making up your mind. Avoid having an attitude about which idea may be the best. Avoid sharing with others which idea you may think is best. Do not compare the ideas in any way.

Is this really a step of its own? Yes, this is a real step. And it might be the most important step. You make sure no one takes a stand. You let no one put themselves in a corner. Ensure there will be no positions to attack or defend. You set them free. Free to discover what they have not yet seen. What they have not yet understood about the new ideas. Free to be open-minded.

Step one must be instructed right from the start. You may need to remind team members about the importance of this step. Remind them as often as needed. It's a reminder not to do what you would normally do: immediately judge. It's a cognitive step. But it has major social impact for the next steps of your idea evaluation.

Step two

Dedicate time to discover potential positive consequences. You look for all positive perspectives on the idea. Do not consider any negatives; keep all negative perspectives out of this step. Introducing negative consequences during this step will risk turning your idea evaluation into a discussion where positives will be weighted directly against negatives. A discussion where you build up positions and decrease curiosity. Keep those negative perspectives out!

It's time to visualize potential future scenarios. What would happen if the idea was to be implemented?

Identify all possible situations that may be affected by the new idea. Produce prototypes for these situations. Visualize the situations on whiteboards. On paper. As a role play. Visualize moment by moment, one interaction at a time, one step at a time, one handling at a time, one action at a time. Like a slow-forward visualization.

Discover all positive aspects as the new idea unfolds in each situation. How will it positively affect your relationships? Your relationships in the team? With other teams? With your customers? How will it positively affect your work routines? Routines around your production? Your logistics? Your sales? Be as specific as possible in visualizing each situation.

Involve people with a nose for good ideas. Involve people to ensure diversity during your visualizing. People that can bring their perspectives and help discover new perspectives on the idea. Facilitate a playful mode of thinking and interacting.

Make sure you fully understand all potential positive consequences that this idea has to offer.

Step three

Now it's time to discover potential negative consequences. Look for all the negative perspectives. This is done in the same way as step two.

Repeat steps two and three

Are you evaluating more ideas? Go through steps two and three for only one idea at a time. Bringing more ideas into steps two and three risks setting the ideas up against each other. Setting the ideas up against each other can lead to strong positioning between team members. This will kill curiosity. It will shut down your open minds. Ideas should be visualized individually.

Pick a random idea. Go through step two. Go through step three. Now, pick the next random idea. Go through steps two and three. Repeat this until you have visualized all ideas under evaluation.

Step four

It's now time to take advantage of all this visualization. Try your best to come up with some alternative ideas. New ideas beyond those originally selected for evaluation. Your visualizations during steps two and three provide an ideal opportunity to mix up these ideas; to see if they can be blended in meaningful new ways; to be turned into a more holistic idea.

You look for ideas that have some of the same positive consequences without having the same negative consequences. If new ideas come about, repeat steps two and three for these ideas too.

After step four, you take a stand on your position; you make up your mind and start having an attitude. You make your final decision. Because now you have been open-minded. You have challenged your own perception. You have tried to get as many deep and wide perspectives as possible. You are ready to make a visionary decision.

Make a good decision. Find the best solution. Be visionary. Creativity gives you a better foundation for decision-making. It ensures that you tackle important and motivating problems. It ensures that you use your imagination to develop a lot of alternative potential ideas. It ensures that you look inquisitively for the potential in each of the novel ideas.

Remember to think about creativity as an alternative to traditional business intelligence: business creativity intelligence. Traditional business intelligence uses analytical thinking. Business creativity intelligence uses creative thinking. They both provide a much better foundation for decision-making.

Traditional business intelligence may be superior for complicated problems in areas with a high level of certainty. Business creativity intelligence may be superior for complex problems in areas with a high level of uncertainty. They will clearly point toward the best solution for the problem. However, creativity cannot make the decision for you.

In the end, you will need to identify and select an idea based on this foundation; an idea that is high on novelty, feasibility, and desirability so that it can help you move forward and so that it is implementable and advantageous. Make your mark on history!

HABIT 4

PERSUASIVE IDEA PRESENTATION

The difference between being considered a weirdo or a genius

Beyond Suggesting Novel Ideas

Want to present your novel idea to colleagues, leaders, users, or customers? Make sure your idea presentation is delivered persuasively.

Too many novel ideas come out as simple suggestions without much persuasive effort. Their value may be vaguely presented, but the entire presentation is often performed with a great deal of hesitation. Hesitation because you are unsure how well the idea will be received. You fear that it may not be welcomed with open arms.

Simply suggesting your novel idea is far too weak. It makes it easy for your audience to instantly reject your idea without reasonable arguments.

You need to take your novel ideas more seriously. Novel ideas may prove to be great ideas as they are tested or implemented. They may become innovative, breakthrough solutions if they get accepted.

Presenting your novel ideas can be tricky. You can present them in an email or a letter, in a live or recorded presentation, on a poster, or in a slideshow.

It's worth making an effort preparing and practicing your idea presentations. This is particularly true when it comes to novel ideas. Novel ideas are harder to grasp for your audience. So you will need to present novel ideas with a great deal of persuasive effort. If your audience doesn't understand your idea, they may think you are a weirdo. **If you get it right, they may consider you a genius.**

Uncertainty

What do you think when others present their novel ideas? Do you worry about how the idea will affect you? Will it make your work harder? Your life tougher?

Novelty creates uncertainty because your audience cannot instantly understand such ideas. Their value isn't clear to the audience. The audience cannot relate a novel idea to previous ideas. It is novel. So it is distinct from previous experience and knowledge. The audience will find it difficult to figure out if the idea will work or not.

Imagine you're working in the shampoo industry. You have come up with an idea for a new type of shampoo. The shampoo is very much like other shampoos. The ingredients are almost like other shampoos. The bottle design is also similar in terms of size and shape. Maybe the shampoo is tweaked a bit to make it smell or look unique.

This new shampoo will be relatively easy to present to an audience. An audience of supermarket procurement officers will know how similar bottles of shampoo generate consistent sales. How, if the price and placement are right, this shampoo could also generate sales in their supermarkets. They feel certain about this, because this new shampoo is like existing shampoos with which they have had experience. If similar shampoos can sell, so can this shampoo. The audience may instantly like the idea without much persuasive effort. They may even accept the idea if conditions and prices are right; if they have bad experiences with similar shampoos, they will probably reject the idea right away.

Now, imagine you have come up with a very different kind of idea for a shampoo. A more novel idea. The bottle design is completely different from other shampoo bottles. It looks more like a big bucket for paint. And the shampoo comes with a "shampoo brush", which is like a paintbrush. You use the shampoo brush to apply the shampoo directly to your hair. Next, you let it dry until it feels like cement in your hair. Now, shake your head. Shake off the dry shampoo. Ta-da. It leaves your hair clean and full of nutrition.

What may go through the mind of your audience?

The bottle seems quite big. Will it fit on the supermarket shelves? Will the supermarket customers even recognize this as a bottle of shampoo? Or will they think it has been misplaced? Will the supermarket staff even understand the shampoo? Will they be able to explain to customers that this is shampoo? And what is this brush about? Will people understand how to use it? Will they steal the brushes? Will they even read the instructions on the bottle? If not, how will they know to let it dry? And how will they know to shake off the shampoo instead of rinsing with water?

All these novel features set this shampoo apart from existing shampoos. It makes it impossible to relate the shampoo to previous experience and knowledge. The audience will not be able to form an opinion about this shampoo. Your audience will be uncertain about its value. Will the supermarket staff make fun of me if I accept this novel type of shampoo bottle? Will my friends hear about this? Will they also laugh at me? Will this be remembered as my biggest procurement mistake ever? I better reject the idea.

Novelty creates uncertainty. Uncertainty leads to fear. Fear makes you want to take the easy way out: reject the idea and move on.

Persuasive idea presentations should help the audience go from uncertainty into a deeper understanding of the value of the novel idea; pointing toward how this new type of shampoo may become a new standard in the shampoo industry or in a niche segment within this industry.

Windows of Opportunity

Novel ideas may create uncertainty. But they also create windows of opportunity. Opportunities to win over your audience. Think about it as a moment of confusion.

Non-novel ideas are less confusing for your audience. They are easy to handle. The idea is easily relatable to previous ideas. Did the previous idea work? If not, this new idea will probably not work either. If yes, this new idea might work, too. The audience will instantly make up their mind.

You see this in political campaigns, in advertising new products and services, in leadership, and in ideas presented in teams. If a new idea is like something you've seen before, you will categorize it accordingly.

If you're a fan of existing Apple products, then you'll tend to be positive toward new products from Apple.

If you are normally supportive of conservative viewpoints, you will tend to be positive toward new conservative ideas as well.

You will likely be critical toward a newly suggested organizational change if this change seems like a previously failed organizational change.

There is a low degree of confusion regarding non-novel ideas. Your audience will make up their minds as they hear about your new idea. Even serious and continuous persuasive efforts will have little effect on your audience's attitude toward such non-novel ideas. Either they like it, or they don't.

This is very different when you are presenting your novel ideas. Novel ideas have the potential to create a lot of confusion. Novel ideas are difficult to categorize according to previous experiences. Your audience may never have seen anything like it. They may have no preconceived attitudes related to your novel idea. This will create a moment of confusion for your audience. The more novel the idea, the higher the degree of confusion. During this moment of confusion, there will be a window of opportunity.

The audience cannot easily make up their mind about your novel idea. So you should present all they need to make up their mind; present a positive first impression.

Point toward the values of your novel idea, the value of its originality, the value of its feasibility, and the value of its desirability. Use persuasive means such as meaningful illustrations and catchphrases. Stage your presentations of your novel ideas.

The window of opportunity is temporary. It may last a few days, a few hours, or it may last just a few minutes. Grab it. Your greatest chance comes when your audience hears about your idea for the first time. That is the best moment to seize your window of opportunity. To make your persuasive presentation of your novel idea. Make sure it's done right.

A Complex Audience

Have you ever tried presenting your novel ideas? Ever been fascinated by just how difficult it is for your audience to support your novel ideas?

Your audience is not just a group of listeners. They are not just people who have to be persuaded. They are far more than a simple a*cceptance* or *rejection* of your novel ideas. They are real people. They are embedded in complex psychological and social constructs. They may have a lot at stake. They may have influence. But this influence may involve a lot of concerns and obligations. There might be a lot of variables involved when your audience decides whether they support or reject your novel idea.

Imagine how Native Americans had to explain to fellow tribe members their experiences with the first European explorers coming to America. Maybe some Native Americans were observing from a distance. Maybe they were hiding in some nearby bushes, observing how the Europeans arrived on their enormous ships. Ships that were much larger than anything they had ever seen before. They may have been surprised by their sails and cannons; surprised by their horses and their armor. It may have been difficult to understand exactly what was going on as the Europeans were riding their horses wearing full shining armor. Everything they saw must have been completely distinct from their previous experiences.

The Native Americans may have tried explaining these new experiences to the tribal chief. They may have been worried about what the Europeans were up to. Maybe they wanted to warn the chief; get him to take action. But the chief of the tribe has a lot at stake.

If the tribal chief believes these novel insights, then other tribal members may cause trouble. They may think he has lost his sense of judgment. Important tribal members may think the chief has gone mad believing in such crazy stories. The tribal chief may even risk a rebellion or an assassination.

Imagine an alien spacecraft landing right in front of you. You see aliens coming out of the spacecraft. See how they look; how they are dressed. Maybe they have brought some animals. How would you explain these experiences to your friends? To your colleagues? There is a high risk that your audience will find it difficult to understand or believe what you're trying to explain. This is very similar to the situation the Native Americans must have experienced.

Keep this mental picture in your mind every time you want to present novel ideas to an audience. You will be in a similar situation as the Native Americans, as if you have seen an alien spacecraft. The idea may be completely clear to you, but your audience may be skeptical toward your novel idea. It could include risks for them to choose to support your idea. They may only accept your novel ideas if they are sure to gain from the idea. Your audience may have certain responsibilities. They may have gained their powerful role because they make good judgments; good decisions. They may have their influential position because they are good at distinguishing between good and bad ideas. And they may lose their power and influence if they support a wrong idea.

Rejection is easier than acceptance. This is true if the audience is unsure about the value and the risks of the idea. Persuasion is about making your audience understand the value and feeling sure about your novel idea.

Go for Gatekeepers

Do you want to get all your colleagues and leaders on board with your novel idea? Want stakeholders to support your novel idea? Want users and customers to support your novel idea? Want operators to comply with your novel idea?

So many audiences need to be persuaded. It may seem overwhelming how many times you will have to present your new idea in order to get it moving; in order to get it tested and implemented.

One audience may be more important than any other audience. This audience has access to significant resources. They have influence over other people's attitudes and opinions. They have the power to open doors for your ideas, doors in your organization, doors in your industry. They can help push your ideas forward. They are the gatekeepers.

Societal gatekeepers decide what is shown on television. What goes on air when it comes to radio. What books are being published. What news stories makes it to the front page. Gatekeepers also make important decisions in politics and finance.

A new type of societal gatekeepers includes social influencers on Instagram, Twitter, YouTube, and TikTok. These gatekeepers have vast amounts of followers they can influence easily. They convey a new message to a broader audience. They make the audience support or comply with new ideas.

Societal gatekeepers may make for quite the interesting audience, but there is another type of gatekeeper that may be far more important. These are the organizational gatekeepers.

Some of them are formal gatekeepers. They sit in important leadership positions. They control the distribution of internal funding and human resources. If they support your idea, you will gain the resources to perform tests and implementation.

Others are informal gatekeepers. They control the unofficial resources. They may have no formal influence, but they have social influence. When they speak, others listen. If they like an idea, others will start to like it too. If they change their way of working, others will follow.

You need to identify relevant gatekeepers. Relevant for your novel idea. They could be on your team, in your department, or in your management. Maybe they are external to your organization, such as a consultancy, supplier, or customer. It could also be a retired employee or leader. Maybe they are not even related directly to your industry.

List gatekeepers that can play a role in getting your idea accepted and gatekeepers that can help provide resources to move forward with your idea.

Next, get these gatekeepers on board. Present your novel idea to them persuasively. Make them see the value of the idea. Make them feel sure about the idea. Get their support, their resources, and their influence.

Succeeding with a novel idea doesn't necessarily mean that you must do all the work yourself. Gatekeepers can help you roll the idea through your team, organization, and beyond. Sometimes gatekeepers take over your idea. They keep pushing the idea forward without you being involved. Do you truly believe the idea is important? Then it doesn't matter who moves the idea forward, whether it's you or a gatekeeper.

No two gatekeepers are the same. And your idea presentations for each gatekeeper should not be the same either. You will need to prepare and practice persuasive idea presentations that match each gatekeeper. That take into account their responsibility, their risks. Then take into account their beliefs and motivation.

Stage Your Idea Presentation

Novel ideas are often reduced to simply being suggestions over a cup of coffee, while walking in the hallway, or during tense meetings. Novel ideas deserve more than an unprepared presentation.

Novel ideas help set your future direction. They push aside declining ideas. They create more valuable solutions. Sometimes they make the difference between a future and no future. You need to set the stage for presenting your novel ideas.

Imagine going to a theater, concert hall, opera, or movie theater. Such places are very good for staging new ideas. The atmosphere. The expectations. The interior. Everything is set up on stage to immerse the audience. The presentations are prepared in detail. To leave the audience with as great an impression as possible. Persuading them about their new idea: the new show.

Remember a great experience at a concert? Now imagine sitting in a cafeteria at work having lunch with some colleagues. Your "great experience" is shown on a screen in the corner of the cafeteria. How will you experience this concert as it is shown on a screen during lunch? Will you have the same great experience as you did in the concert hall?

You may be in a cognitive competition, trying to watch the screen while chatting with your colleagues, eating your lunch, being disturbed by colleagues greeting you as they walk past your table, answering text messages on your phone, checking the news and sport results, being irritated by noises from moving chairs and bad acoustics, or thinking about the next meeting that starts right after lunch. It may not be the same great experience to watch the show in the cafeteria.

Lots of ideas are shared randomly during lunch in cafeterias. Ideas are shared during meetings where other urgent matters get all the attention. Ideas are shared during social chats where small-talk topics may be favored over thought-provoking ideas. Presenting novel ideas doesn't stand a chance in such settings. They need a setting dedicated to immersing the audience in the novel ideas; a setting with no other matters on the agenda. With no disturbances that can take away attention.

Novel ideas are vulnerable. There are few convenient times for presenting such ideas during normal workdays. You are constantly in efficiency mode. You want to get things done; to get through your to-do lists. And novel ideas rarely tick off urgent tasks on your to-do lists. It just feels better getting urgent tasks done than starting up on a big new idea. You need to set the stage to help your novel ideas win against these favored to-do lists.

There are several means for communicating novel ideas: videos, poster, emails, oral presentations, booklets, etc. It is important to separate your idea presentation from other matters, regardless of your means of communication. It may be possible to reserve a special room for idea presentations. You may invite your audience to an external meeting setting when presenting novel ideas. A setting where your audience can leave behind the daily hustle and stress; leave aside computers, tablets, and phones; leave aside other matters; leave aside the to-do lists.

Stage your idea presentation like a concert at a concert hall. Make your own "idea hall." Set expectations. Make sure your audience knows how much effort you have put into coming up with the novel idea and how much effort you have put into preparing your idea presentation. Create a serious, yet relaxed and fun, atmosphere for your idea presentation.

Make It Memorable

You need to attract your audience's attention to create a memorable understanding about your new idea.

A progress bar is one way to help create such a memorable understanding. Progress bars can help your audience understand how your idea may fit into a long-term organizational evolution. Or into a long-term industrial evolution. How your idea can take you one step forward in this evolution. Take you from level three to level four or level up from a fifth-generation way of thinking to a sixth-generation way of thinking. A progress bar suggests that you are already moving forward in the path of evolution. It suggests how you will have to continue moving forward. That this idea can help you move forward to get to the next level. Use specific numbers, statistics, and graphs directly related to the key features of the idea. Use them to highlight expected effects of going from your current level to the next level.

Authority is a strong, persuasive principle that can also help make your ideas more memorable. Get support from authoritative people. It could be a leader, a domain expert, or maybe even a famous person. Make sure they understand your novel idea. Make them express some type of support for your idea. Use quotes, pictures, or illustrations to present these authorities and their expression of support for your novel idea. It is easier for your audience to support your idea if they see that authoritative people have already expressed their support.

Humor is another strong persuasive principle. However, it's not enough to simply crack a random joke at random times during your idea presentation. You will need to integrate the humorous aspect directly into a key point of your novel idea. It must relate to one of the most important points you want your audience to understand and remember. Avoid political and sexual humor. Keep the humorous aspect as universal as possible. Humor can be integrated as text, pictures, or illustrations.

Metaphors and analogies create strong mental images that are easy to remember. Develop a metaphor or an analogy related to a key point of your idea. You may want to present an exclusive new type of burger: "The Ferrari Burger". You may want to present an idea for a new private garden camping concept: "The Airbnb for camping".

Metaphors and analogies can be designed to create a strong emotional connection between the audience and your idea. You will need to identify important emotional triggers. Triggers that are likely to have a strong effect on your audience. These may include wellness, beauty, mental peace, and mass slaughter. Now, connect these triggers with key points of your idea. If you want to convince your friend to take sleep more seriously: "Sleep is beauty in the making." If you want to invite a friend out for a beer: "Beer is peace of mind." If you want to convince your friend to join a "Save the Trees" demonstration: "They are mass slaughtering our trees." And if you want to suggest a new meeting structure for your colleagues: "Our meetings will finally become an oasis for mental peace." Create your own metaphors and analogies directly related to your idea.

Include rhythm in key messages of your novel idea. "Cheese is good for your neighborhood." "We create borders by using natural waters." Rhythm makes catchphrases memorable. It makes them even more catchy. Put together meaningful catchphrases that rhyme. Put some effort into it. Be playful.

You may also consider other persuasive principles. Use moral appeal to point toward fundamental beliefs about right and wrong in your idea. Use beauty appeal to attract attention toward specific details in your idea. Use powerful words directly related to key values in the idea, such as undoubtedly, enormous, fascinating, fantastic, tempting, and brilliant. Design personalized messages for your audience. Develop an appealing name for your idea.

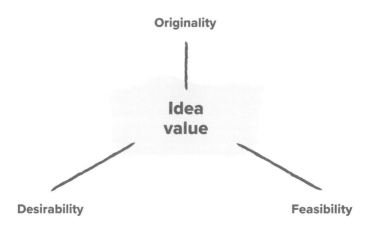

To win over your audience, you will need to place strong emphasis on the relevant values related to your novel ideas. The value of originality, feasibility, and desirability. You will need to do so in a sound and convincing way.

Idea Originality

You need to present clearly what is original about your new ideas. What is unique. What makes this idea so special? In what way does it have innovative potential? Potential to set new standards in your team and industry? Potential to lead to a breakthrough solution for one of your important problems?

You can point toward how recent changes in your team or industry have created a new situation. It may be due to the introduction of new technology, a new type of collaboration, new regulations, new employees, societal changes, or changes in market demands. Changes that call for a new type of solution. This creates the possibility to compare the *old reality* with the *new reality*. To illustrate, quantify and qualify the differences between how it was before and how it has become. Or how it will likely become in the near future. You will need to explain how your novel idea matches with this new reality, how it fits the new situation, how it can help your team follow up on these recent changes.

Future scenarios are powerful in making the audience understand the difference between old reality and new reality. They show how the idea meets unseen, yet plausible, future needs. Present scenarios of how the idea may positively affect your team and industry once implemented. What effects do you see after two days? After two months? After two years? Future scenarios can also reveal how your novel idea may have other positive effects in your organization and industry. Positive effects that go beyond the problem you want to solve. As such, the novel idea can help your team develop a new understanding about yourself, your work, your organization, and your industry.

Novel ideas create uncertainty. But uncertainty is okay if credibility is high. Point toward the credibility of the novel idea. Transparency is key. It creates trustworthiness. Transparency into your creative efforts, your rigorous exploration of problem areas, your exhaustive work on idea combinations and fearless elaborations, and your open-minded visionary idea evaluations. Make your audience comprehend your creative efforts. Let them know about the forty other ideas you have worked on. Let them understand why this final idea is better than all these other ideas. A researcher presents their research method to create credibility for their research results. Likewise, you need to present your creative method to create credibility for your creative results.

The creative team can also transfer credibility toward the novel idea. Point toward the team's creative experience. How the team has previously succeeded in coming up with valuable ideas. How the team involves expertise in areas relevant for the problem and the novel idea. And how you involved other relevant users, industry experts, and idea experts in the development and evaluation of this idea. Your team and your creative efforts can help legitimize the originality of your new idea.

Original ideas are key ingredients for innovation. They are also key ingredients for new learning. You can point toward the need to try out new ideas to create a culture of learning. To take a chance on innovation. To move forward despite uncertainty. You can never be 100% sure about the success of novel ideas. You cannot predict the future. Yet, you must step into it. Novel ideas are potential steps into the future. They will always include a degree of chance. Do you call yourself an innovator? Then you will sometimes need to try out novel ideas. It will also send a signal that you take innovation seriously. That you dare to go for originality.

Make it clear to your audience how motivated you are about this novel idea. Show how you are ready to take the idea through the next steps. That you will take responsibility for these next steps. Trying out the idea as a test or an experiment. Show that you are willing to spend the necessary time and resources on this idea. Show your dedication for the idea. Point toward how you need their help. That you need help from the audience to move forward. If your audience believes in you, it will be easier for them to support your idea.

Idea Feasibility

You need to present the realizability of your novel ideas clearly. How easily will your new idea be implemented? How can it be accomplished? The feasibility of this idea may be obvious to you, but for your audience it could be hard to grasp exactly what it will take for your novel idea to succeed. Any novel idea can seem complicated the first time you hear about it.

You can present the idea implementation as a series of smaller steps. Show how each step takes you closer to the realization of the idea. Make each step seem affordable and easy to understand. Explain how the first steps can be performed without much effort. Without much cost. How these first steps involve tests and experiments that can reveal a lot more about the idea's potential. And a lot more about the idea's feasibility. Focus specifically on the first few steps rather than going through an exhaustive presentation of all the necessary steps of your full implementation plan.

The first idea presentation will rarely lead to a full acceptance of your new idea. This is particularly true for novel ideas. They don't just get instant full backing. Your audience may not get the full picture the first time. But they may like the idea enough to support it for a while. Try to think about it as an iterative process. You present your idea, you get temporary support, you present again, you get more support to move on, and so forth, until the idea is fully implemented. In each idea presentation, you will need to gain access to resources until you reach the next step. Show your audience that you are ready to take the next step today. That you are motivated to get started right now.

Present an expensive and complex alternative to your novel idea. This will make your real idea seem cheaper and more feasible. Some ideas are objectively unfeasible. They may go against the laws of physics. Or maybe they're harmful to people. However, for most ideas, feasibility is rather a matter of relativity. How easy or how difficult will it be to implement your new idea? The audience will find it easier to place your novel idea on a relative feasibility scale if they have an alternative idea for comparison. Make sure this alternative idea will make your novel idea seem more feasible. Make it seem like a piece of cake.

Present the obvious flaws in your idea. Your audience will most likely see them anyway. Make it clear that you are completely aware of these flaws. Explain how you intend to handle these flaws. This will make it easier to present the true value of your idea without your audience constantly focusing on these potential flaws. They will feel more at ease with the flaws and will be able to immerse themselves more easily into the benefits of your idea.

You can point toward how the idea is feasibly related to beliefs or expectations for the future. How the idea fits perfectly into your ambition, vision, or strategy. How the idea is consistent with previous statements in your organization: "You always talk about the importance of ... Now, I will present you with an idea that can do just that." You like to be consistent with your beliefs. You like to be consistent with your previous statements, especially if these were expressed with a great deal of determination. **Look for strong statements previously made by your audience.** Point toward how your idea can help turn those statements into reality.

Idea Desirability

"Why have we never thought about this before?"

"How did we live without this?"

That's the feeling you want to leave with your audience. What is particularly desirable about your novel idea? Whom does the idea benefit? The audience themselves? Colleagues? Stakeholders? Users? Customers? And more importantly—how does it benefit those people?

You may point toward specific beneficiaries. State their specific names. Show pictures of them. State the name of their department, organization, and geographical location. Describe the specific situations where these specific people will benefit from your novel idea. Use pictures or video to make these situations come alive for your audience. Develop a prototype to give a realistic feeling of the idea. A prototype may be a product, a website, an illustration, or a video showing the idea as if it were already implemented.

Consider instructing a role play as part of your idea presentation. To make your audience experience being in the shoes of the beneficiaries. Role plays can create compelling real-life-like experiences of novel ideas, awakening real emotions in your audience. You may decorate your presentation room to make it feel like a beneficiary situation. If the idea provides key benefits to a checkout situation in a supermarket, turn the presentation room into a supermarket checkout situation. You may prepare a role play script that will take your audience through a future scenario experiencing the benefits of the ideas. They get to experience it as if they were the beneficiaries.

Role plays are risky. They need to be well prepared. They can be fun, but the audience should never be left feeling silly. It should be as close to a real-life experience as possible. Make sure you have necessary decorations and equipment to provide a proper experience for your audience. You may play a role in the role play. You may also involve outsiders to join the role play. However, it's essential that the audience has the insightful experience themselves. Let the audience play the central roles in your role play.

The obvious way is to present how the beneficiaries will come to benefit from your idea. But you can also turn it upside down. You can stress the risk of not implementing your novel idea. Imagine a toothbrush advertisement telling you how you risk getting tooth cavities if you don't upgrade to a new toothbrush. Make it clear what they stand to lose if the idea is not implemented. Maybe you can present your novel idea by pointing toward how bad things will be without it.

Try to create a feeling of grouping for your audience. Make them understand how others have already implemented a similar idea; other audiences, other decision makers in other teams, in other companies, in competing companies. Make your audience understand how they are in a comparable situation. How, accepting your idea will just be doing what most others have already done. If all these others have accepted a similar idea, then your audience is not alone in doing the same. Getting your audience to feel as if they are part of a bigger group can help boost their belief in your idea. Their confidence to support your novel idea. Be as specific as possible. Specify who these "others" are. Specify when they accepted these similar ideas.

You may also use prior positive benchmarking. Pretend as if you already expect your audience to accept your idea. That you expect their support because it would be the right thing to do. "You want the best for our users, right? Any responsible person would support this idea. I presume you support the idea too. Let's go forward with this idea, right?" Point toward how others will start imitating your novel idea once it will be implemented. How it will become a benchmark for others. That others will look at your idea as inspiration.

Ethical Considerations

Novel ideas have the potential to change the way people think. The way they behave. The way they interact. When implemented, novel ideas have the potential to lead to breakthrough solutions. Solutions that impact people inside and outside of your organization and industry.

Novel ideas are difficult for your audience to understand. It is hard for them to fully grasp potential negative effects of such ideas. Persuasive idea presentations make it even harder for your audience to identify potential ethical dilemmas.

As the creator of the idea, you have the advantage of understanding the idea best. You need to use this advantage to **make serious ethical considerations before revealing your idea to your audience.** You need to make the hard choice of whether the idea should be presented at all. You have the responsibility of sharing potential risks in relation to your idea presentation.

Is the idea fundamentally good? Not just good for you, but also good for the people who must implement it? Good for your organization, good for the beneficiaries, good for the industry, good for your stakeholders, good for society, and good for humanity? Do you truly believe this is a good idea? Is it more about you getting a reward from your leader? Or about getting respect for your creative efforts?

Your idea may follow a trend in your organization and industry. That doesn't necessarily mean that it's a good idea. You need to consider ethical dimensions of your idea regardless of how existing solutions may seem like your new idea. Other creators may have made ethical mistakes in the past. You must do it right.

Map everyone likely to be affected directly and indirectly by your novel idea. Identify how each of them is likely to be affected in case your idea is implemented. Maybe you can elaborate on the idea to cause less harm. Otherwise, you may need to include details about potential harmful effects in your idea presentation.

Pay attention to the ethical considerations throughout your problem understanding, idea production, and idea evaluation. The most important ethical considerations may be related to the preparation of your persuasive idea presentation. When you start to persuade your audience to accept your idea, to support your idea, to comply with your idea. Once important gatekeepers have accepted your idea, it can be difficult to take back the idea. Make sure the idea and your idea presentation have been through some rigorous ethical considerations. Be extra rigorous for ideas that involve high risks related to important matters like health and finances. And be extra cautious about ethical dilemmas for idea presentations targeting vulnerable audiences like children, the poor, the sick, the elderly, the mentally ill, and people who have recently lost a loved one.

Four-Step Idea Presentation

Persuasion may make the difference between being considered a weirdo and being considered a genius. You need to invest dedicated effort into preparing a persuasive presentation to increase the chance that your idea will be accepted and supported.

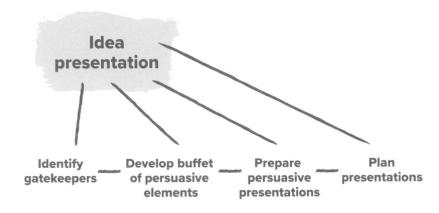

Let's go through a four-step model for preparing a persuasive idea presentation.

Step one

Identify important gatekeepers to support your idea. Gatekeepers with relevant influence and resources. Look for both formal and informal gatekeepers. Look inside and outside your organization and industry. Make a list of these gatekeepers.

For each gatekeeper, identify their motivation. Their responsibility. Their beliefs. Consider these gatekeepers to be your first line of persuasion.

Identify and list all other people you need to persuade, such as relevant colleagues, leaders, users, customers, stakeholders, etc.

Step two

Identify alternative persuasive values related to originality, feasibility, and desirability. Come up with memorable illustrations, catchphrases, and other persuasive means. Use persuasive principles as inspiration. You may also use historically important persuasive messages as inspiration, such as political speeches, advertisements, communication campaigns, etc. Come up with as many alternative persuasive texts, illustrations, and catchphrases as possible.

Step three

Consider the output from step two as a buffet of persuasive elements. Select and combine meaningful persuasive elements into your final persuasive idea presentations. Each presentation should be customized to fit its unique audience. You may include emails, posters, videos, prototypes, role plays, oral presentations, and any other media. Consider ethical dilemmas for each idea presentation.

Step four

Plan where and when to deliver each idea presentation for each audience. It's all about timing. Remember to stage your idea. Once you start persuading your audience, the idea will be floating around on its own. Maybe your audience will start talking about your idea; telling your idea to others. Suddenly, your idea may be everywhere.

Remember how there are short windows of opportunities for novel ideas? You need to grab these opportunities while the window is open. However, if the idea is shared randomly near and far, then you may not be able to make a persuasive first impression of your idea to all important gatekeepers.

If you fail to persuade important gatekeepers, they may not use their influence and resources to support your idea. This can make it more difficult to move forward with your idea. If important gatekeepers accept your idea, they will likely support your idea toward implementation.

Plan your idea presentations so you are sure to reach all important gatekeepers with a persuasive idea presentation. The presentation may not necessarily be delivered by you, personally. But it must be persuasive regardless. Make sure of that!

KICK-START YOUR CREATIVITY JOURNEY

Turn your team into
an idea machine

Are You Creative Yet?

I once co-designed a master's level university course on creativity. A course that wouldn't just teach participants about creativity. Rather, this course would make participants far more creative in their professional work and in their area of study. I developed and taught the course for seven consecutive years in collaboration with Søren Hansen. For ordinary university students, the course workload was equivalent to six months of full-time study. For professional participants, the workload was equivalent to twelve months of part-time study.

It attracted participants from more than forty different industries and from more than thirty different study programs, internationally. For most participants, creative skills and confidence were already above average prior to joining the course. And almost every participant could be characterized as highly open toward new experiences. Even without this course on creativity, such a group would seem ideal for making instant successful creative efforts. Yet, every single year, participants were disappointed with their initial creative efforts during the first day of the course.

The first week of the course was designed to perform what some participants termed as "a reconfiguration of the mind." It was an upgrade to IQ2. IQ version 2.0. Or rather, an upgrade of CQ. To let the participants experience using their creativity quotient. To learn about their creative efforts in practice.

Participants were instructed to solve a series of problems creatively —both individually and in small teams. On the first day, all such creative efforts were documented by video recordings, audio recordings, and written notes.

Later, as the participants learned about important creative skills, they were instructed to analyze these videos, audios, and notes to understand their creative efforts on the first day of the course better.

How good were they at creative problem understanding? Did they go beyond standard problem-solving? Were they able to challenge fundamental standards? Did they explore the problem area, developing alternative well-defined sub-problems? Did they end up choosing problems that were both meaningful, motivating, and interesting?

How good were they at idea production? Did they go beyond viable solutions and initial patterns of thinking? How many alternative ideas were they able to produce? How many of these ideas were surprisingly novel? How often did they elaborate on each other's ideas? Elaborate on novel ideas before judging them as too wild?

How good were they at idea evaluation? Did they go beyond standard evaluation? Did they end up using discussion, creating strong positions, and favoring old ideas? Were they curious and open-minded toward ideas that challenged their own perception? Ideas that offered an opportunity to look for new perspectives? Did they end up with a novel solution for their problems?

How good were they at idea presentation? Did they go beyond simple idea suggestions? Were they able to make memorable expressions of their ideas? Were they able to point toward values like originality, feasibility, and desirability? Were they able to use persuasive means as part of their idea presentations? Did they identify any ethical dilemmas related to their ideas or their idea presentations?

This analysis helped the participants develop a stronger understanding about their creative efforts. By analyzing their creative production, they were able to gain insight into their creative abilities. It didn't give a full picture of their creative nature. However, it did reveal a lot about their creative efforts. It gave details about how creative they were able to be when asked to be creative.

Do you understand your own creative efforts? Do you have a clear picture of your team's creative performance? Most people have a vague feeling about their creative efforts. However, this feeling is often based on the creative experience, not on the creative production. You feel creative when energies are high. When ideas are shared across the table in a fun and playful way. But have you ever analyzed your actual creative production? Set the feelings aside, look at the raw ideas. You may be surprised.

Try documenting your creative efforts. Record your creativity meetings, brainstorming sessions, and innovative workshops. Record management meetings. Especially meetings where important decisions are being made. You may also set up a simulated innovative challenge. One that is not directly related to your everyday work tasks. Record yourself being creative during this challenge. Go through these recordings to analyze your creative efforts.

Get a notebook. Digital or physical. Make notes of all your ideas. You may already have your previous ideas documented somewhere. Do you have an archive of deviation reports? Of problem-solving sessions? Or an archive of previous innovative projects? Go through these archives to analyze your previous creative efforts.

Creative Self-Perception

How do you see yourself as a creative person? Do you believe in your own creative potential? Do you trust your creativity to come alive when you want it to? When creativity is truly needed? Or is it more like this random thing that seems to appear from out of the blue, sometimes even when it is no longer needed?

Let's look at your creative self-perception.

The key is to ask yourself fundamental questions related to creative thinking, behavior, and interaction. Your answers may help reveal how you perceive your own creative potential. This type of insight can help you decide whether you or your team may need to develop some creative skills to boost your creative confidence.

Ask yourself the following questions. Rate your response on a scale from one to ten. Or create a deeper reflection leading to an elaborate description including examples of when, where, how, and in which situations you consider yourself creative.

Can you come up with more alternative ideas than what most others are capable of? Are you one of those who just keeps coming up with new ideas?

Are you often asked to help colleagues and friends come up with new ideas for their problems? Help them get ideas they never thought about themselves? Do other people consider you a creative inspiration for their work?

Do you often go for the novel ideas, even if you've got some other really good ideas? Do you look specifically for those surprising ideas? Ideas that can challenge your current ideas. Do you find it more interesting to elaborate on wild ideas?

Do you sometimes get so immersed in ideas that you completely forget about time? Forgetting about all the other important tasks you needed to do today?

Are you aware of dominating patterns in your way of thinking? Do you notice them daily? Notice them when you are trying to produce new ideas? These patterns may be formed from ideas shared early in a meeting. Or they may be based on current logic in your team.

Are you curious about ideas that challenge your way of thinking? Ideas from other people? Ideas that are different from your perspective? Are you open-minded toward different ways to handle familiar situations? Do you get inspired hearing about them?

Do you like to look for potential positive and negative consequences of an idea before making up your mind? Do you suspend judgment until you have fully understood all alternative ideas? Do you look for potential in behavior and ideas that you don't clearly understand? Do you look for alternative explanations for strange ideas and behavior?

Do you consider opposing ideas as perfect opportunities for new learnings? Do you like to challenge your own perspectives and understandings about problems and ideas?

Do you like to work on complex problems? Trying to challenge what most others would normally take for granted?

Are you confident presenting your novel ideas to your colleagues? To your leader? To all kinds of audiences? Are you good at pointing toward new values of your novel ideas? Do you have a good feeling about your audience's values, responsibility, and motivation?

Do you know a structured approach for being creative? How to produce multiple ideas at will and on command? How to develop deeper problem understanding? How to evaluate new ideas? How to prepare persuasive idea presentations? Will you be able to explain details about this systematic approach to others?

Do you wish your answers to the above questions were different? Maybe you should consider developing your creative skills and boosting your creative confidence.

Creative Team Culture

I once worked with a defense academy. It was a complex setting involving members of the army, the navy, and the air force. They wanted more innovative solutions proposed as part of their daily work. They wanted to be able to turn all their knowledge into potential new solutions; to be able to apply previous experiences to solve novel situations. Experience and knowledge from their military training as well as from their general lives. An unlimited application of knowledge and experience to solve complex situations. We called this *creativity on command*.

They needed to build a creative team culture. A culture based on inspiration. A culture that brought out creative thinking and behavior from across the team. Where everyone dared to share their ideas. And where everyone felt the importance of sharing their ideas for the greater good of the entire team. We started off making a baseline status for their current creative culture before assessing how to further nurture creativity in their team.

You, too, can make a baseline status for your current creative culture. To gain a better understanding as to whether and what kind of nurture would make sense for your team.

The key is to make serious team reflections on important matters related to your creative culture.

Do you have effective formal (or informal) procedures for how to be creative as a team? Does everyone know about these procedures? Does everyone understand them and have experience in how to follow these procedures? Do you have someone competent in facilitating your team according to these creative procedures?

Do you feel a degree of hesitation when beginning complex problem-solving? Do you feel confident taking on these types of problems? Is your entire team engaged? Is your work on such problems mostly characterized by concentration and motivation? Or is it rather characterized by confusion and irritation?

Is there a positive attitude toward new ideas? Are ideas listened to? Are they taken seriously? Even the wild ideas? Is there a fear of criticism? Fear of losing face if someone makes a joke out of a new idea? Is there encouragement to share ideas in the team? Do you have an expectation that everyone contributes with all their ideas?

Do you try out new ideas for the sake of learning and innovation? To see what happens when you experiment with new ideas? Do you try out novel ideas in a "sandbox" environment? Is there a general curious attitude toward what happens when new ideas are being tested? Are mistakes punished? Or are they seen as part of your new learnings?

Do you have continuous motivation to look for better solutions? Are you in constant pursuit of more effective and valuable solutions? Are you unsettled until you reach a final, never-changing, rock-solid solution? Or do you enjoy your innovative development as a never-ending process of discovery?

Do you prioritize creative efforts with time and resources? More time for important problems? Do you feel a pressure to make decisions quickly?

Are your creative efforts characterized by relaxed and playful sessions? Or are they characterized more so by shorter relatively stressful sessions?

Boost Your Creative Confidence

I once worked with the mayor's office of a large municipality. They wanted to become far more creative. They had already attended several courses on world-famous creativity tools and innovative process methods. They were experts in preparing, facilitating, and performing effective creativity meetings and workshops. If they needed to solve a problem creatively, they were able to come up with novel and valuable solutions within temporary environments. They could schedule a creativity meeting on Friday from 10 a.m. until noon. Or an innovative workshop from Monday to Wednesday, six hours a day. They were experts in the temporary enhancement of creative efforts.

They wanted to go beyond creativity tools and process methods. They wanted to go beyond temporary enhancement of creative efforts. They wanted to wake up in the morning being naturally creative, whenever and for whatever creativity was needed.

Creativity should no longer be just a method or a tool. No longer just creativity workshops or meetings. They wanted creativity to be an attitude. Second nature. They wanted creative problem-solving to become completely natural to them; to be "nothing special." That creativity would become just like any other work-related skill set. They wanted creativity to be so natural that it would feel like eating problems for breakfast. So we designed a creativity fitness center.

The fitness center was designed for exercising fundamental creative skills. To boost creative confidence. We never talked about theories of creativity. We never talked about creativity tools or creative methods. Instead, we practiced being creative. Being creative as individuals. And being creative as teams. We performed hundreds of creativity exercises to turn creativity into a new habit. Or rather, into four creative habits.

What? A fitness center for creativity? Exercising your way to become more creative? What is this all about?

Practicing Creativity

How do you develop a skill? How do you build confidence related to a skill set?

Let's look at math skills. We practice the numbers. We practice counting. We practice addition, subtraction, multiplication, and division. We practice the multiplication tables. We practice geometry. We practice over and over how to draw a perfect circle. We don't just learn about these mathematical concepts. We practice them. We learn them by heart.

In sports, it is not enough to discuss your football match over a pint of beer. It is not enough to watch lots of televised football matches. That doesn't make you a good football player. You need to practice how to throw the ball. How to pass the ball. How to kick the ball. Your coach will take you through specific exercises for you to develop into a skilled and confident football player. Your coach will select exercises that take you to your next development zone. You will not just do what you do best. The exercises will help you discover new and more meaningful ways to play football. You will expand your comfort zone. You will become a more holistically skilled football player. A better football player.

The same is true for creativity. It is not enough to read a book about creativity. It's not enough to watch a keynote speech or some videos about creativity. It's not enough to discuss creativity over a cup of coffee. You will need to practice creativity. To practice fundamental creative skills repeatedly. Until they stick. Until you become confident using them whenever and for whatever problems or situations you may encounter. That's when creativity becomes second nature to you. To your team. It will be your new creative habit. You will have gained a new innovative capability. You are en route to break away from a culture of conformity. En route toward a culture of originality.

Some people consider creativity only as a tool. As a process method; as a temporary special environment or an organizational structure. Some consider creativity as a natural gift, awarded to those few who work in the creative industries. They look at creativity from a rather binary point of view—you either have it, or you don't. If you cannot see creativity as a skill set, then you will not understand the need for practice. Realizing that creativity is also a skill set may be your missing link for succeeding on your creativity journey.

Your Creativity Fitness Center

It is no quick fix. A traditional fitness center does not instantly build muscles. It does not lead to improved cardiovascular functions overnight. It doesn't suddenly change your physical condition. It takes time and commitment. The same is the case for your creativity fitness center. Building skills and confidence takes time. That's why it's called a creativity journey. Little by little, you'll become more creative.

The good news is that you'll feel a difference after just a few hours of exercising creativity. You will quickly gain a real experience with your creative skills. You will experience your colleagues as creative human beings. You will experience how they have interesting ideas. How they are suddenly far more open-minded. How you can play with novel and interesting ideas together. You will feel a difference all the way through your creativity journey.

Imagine learning to ride a bike. At first, you cannot even stay on the bike. You fall over again and again. After about one or two hours, you will be able to balance. To stay on the bike. After a few more hours, you may dare biking on public streets. Eventually, you will be confident biking to school or work. Still, you will have room for improvement. If you want to join the Tour de France, you may have to continue practicing for years. The same is the case for creativity.

At first, you may feel a bit confused. Will you be able to be creative at all? Will you understand the exercises? Will you be able to contribute creatively when practicing with your colleagues? This confusion is normal. As with any new skills, you will need to go through these first steps of practice before gaining the first level of confidence. Soon, you will be better. It's important that this first period of practice is conducted in a "sandbox" environment. Complete the exercises in smaller groups. Have no expectations for creative output. Do not share your ideas outside of the practice context. Make it a safe, fun, and relaxed space for practicing creativity.

After a while, you will feel more confident. The exercises will seem easier. They will also become more interesting and fun to practice. This is because you will start producing more of those surprisingly novel ideas. Ideas that are new to you and your team. You may begin to think of the exercises as simple tools and methods. You will be able to use these tools and methods in all sorts of situations beyond the fitness center. Please do so. It will help you become even more skilled and confident. You will need to continue the practice from here. It should not just be a simple tool kit. You need to keep on developing some good creative habits. Keep the "sandbox" environment for the practice context. Enjoy the practice.

Eventually, you will feel that some of the exercises become too easy. That's not necessarily because the exercises are getting easier. Rather, it is you becoming better; becoming more creative! Creativity is becoming more natural to you. Continue the practice but scale down the intensity of your exercise sessions.

Use your improved creative skills to take the exercises to a higher level. Get far more ideas and far more novel ideas during your practice. Go to higher levels of curiosity. Look for more difficult standards to challenge. Make your ideas even more persuasive. You are not at the end of your journey yet.

When do you stop practicing your creativity? Well, it depends on your ambitions. What are your ambitions for creativity? Do you want the confidence to be more creative in your daily work? To perform better during innovative processes? Do you want a more open-minded team culture? Do you want a more perseverant attitude toward complex problems? Do you need creative confidence to come up with breakthrough novel solutions? Or do you want to become an influential innovator in your industry? To join the Tour de France of innovation?

You may choose to evaluate your creative efforts, your creative self-perception, and your creative team culture. These evaluations give insights into the progress of your creativity journey. You may use them at specific intervals during your creativity journey, but beware of measuring your progress all the time. Make sure the fitness center is based on creative "sandbox" experiences. You will find it hard to progress if you are constantly focusing on your creative output, skills, and confidence. You need to focus on the creative experience, not the creative output. The creative output will improve as your skills and confidence develop. A farmer doesn't dig up his seed every other week to check how much it has grown. Have patience. Let the creativity exercises become real creative experiences. This will foster a more stable journey.

Creativity Exercises

What are the exercises that help develop creative skills and confidence? What are they all about?

The exercises should facilitate a series of challenging and successful creative experiences. Creativity exercises must give you real experiences in how to be creative, both individually and as a team. They must be challenging, but not hard. They should be challenging in order to expand your creative skills. Take you to the next level. Develop creative skills that you may not be so confident in yet. And they must lead to a self-perceived successful creative performance. This is what boosts your creative confidence. If the exercise makes you feel like a failure, it risks worsening your creative confidence.

It's possible to categorize creativity exercises into two dimensions. In one dimension, you have the exercise context. The context may be from everyday problem areas. It may be a professional context like sales, leadership, research, logistics, product design, production, quality control, or business development. Or it may be a societal context, addressing fundamental problem areas in society.

In the other dimension, you have the problem area. Each type of exercise can be designed as a general problem area or as a personal problem area. Personal problem areas come from your personal life, your personal work, your team's work. They may even be real problems you need to solve anyway as part of your daily work. Or problems that you have previously tried to solve.

Personal problem areas are highly motivating to work on. But they are also harder to solve creatively. It's harder to create the "sandbox" playful environment when the problems are real. You may fear that your ideas will be judged as crazy thinking. Fear that your colleagues may think that you are unqualified for your job because you suggest some novel ideas that they cannot understand. Suddenly, the creative exercise will be about "keeping up appearances," and this kills creativity.

The fear of judgment from colleagues can make it difficult to have successful creative experiences for these types of exercises. Therefore, it is a good idea to start off practicing your creative skills on general problem areas. Problem areas that are not personalized. Problem areas in which there is no need to prove yourself. Problem areas where everyone is equal. Everyone can be creative about a random supermarket or a random shoe. Exercises based on general problem areas can give you a quicker initial boost of creative confidence. As your creative confidence increases, you may include more exercises that are based on personal problem areas.

Everyday Exercises

What are everyday problem areas? And how can they be used as cases for creativity exercises? Well, think about what you do during a normal day.

You wake up: Come up with ideas for a new type of alarm clock. Or challenge the standard mattress.

You take a shower: Challenge the standard shower head. Or come up with ideas for a new type of shampoo.

You go to work: Come up with new ways to communicate with nearby cars in congested traffic. Or challenge standard car entertainment.

You go shopping: Challenge the standard customer service in a clothing store. Or come up with ideas for new shopping mall services for children.

It's hard to be creative about problems that you do not clearly understand. Not everyone can challenge standards related to space rocket engines. It doesn't mean that they are less creative human beings. It just means that they don't have any primary experiences related to space rocket engines. Or they don't have knowledge about this problem area. If they had such knowledge or experience, they could be creative about space rocket engines. That's why everyday problems areas are brilliant for exercising creativity. Everyone has some degree of experience and knowledge with everyday problem areas.

Have you ever been to the hairdresser? Then you will be able to identify some relevant problems related to hairdressing. And you will be able to be creative about them. Most people have primary experiences related to supermarkets, shoes, clothing stores, coffee cups, schools, bikes, social conflicts, phone calls, news, voting, chairs, showering, sports, birthday parties, bus stops, bakeries, window cleaning, dentists, elderly care, nursing, books, cars, gardening, restaurants, cooking, fishing, dancing, concerts, fast food, makeup, computers, painting, museums, kitchen pots, balloons, combs, calendars, magnets, pens, tools, movie theaters, toilets, washing hands, door handles, and refrigerators. Do you have experience or knowledge about these everyday problem areas? If yes, then they'll provide good problem areas for your creativity exercises.

Practicing exploration

Let's go through some everyday creativity exercises that can help boost your creative confidence related to exploration and problem understanding.

Movie theaters often place their guests facing the same direction. Challenge whether it must be this way. Could there be other ways?

Generate problem definitions related to washing hands in restrooms. Search for functions, interactions, and objects related to this problem area. Turn ill-defined problems into several well-defined sub-problems.

Challenge the standard way of welcoming children in a kindergarten. Question whether it must be this way. Could there be other ways?

Generate problem definitions related to a kitchen refrigerator. Search for functions, interactions, and objects related to this problem area. Turn ill-defined problems into several well-defined sub-problems.

Challenge the traditional garden barbecue. Question whether it must be this way. Could there be other ways?

Generate problem definitions related to the use of public parks during rainy days. Search for functions, interactions, and objects related to this problem area. Turn ill-defined problems into several well-defined sub-problems.

Practicing imagination

Next, let's look at a few everyday creativity exercises that can help boost your creative confidence related to imagination and idea production.

Develop ideas for new ways car drivers can find free parking spaces. Use inspiration from other situations that also need to produce an overview of free resources.

Develop ideas for rethinking a movie theater. Use inspiration from a sports coach, arts dealer, garbage bin, and museum to create new idea combinations.

Develop ideas for new ways to serve ice cream scoops. Use inspiration from other situations where it is possible to mix and match.

Develop ideas for rethinking a clothing store. Use inspiration from a bus driver, prison, politician, and mine worker to create new idea combinations.

Develop ideas for rethinking a toothbrush. Use inspiration from other situations where curved surfaces need to be cleaned.

Develop ideas for rethinking a baby stroller. Use inspiration from a journalist, bricklayer, rubber band, and tennis racket to create new idea combinations.

Practicing curiosity

Now, let's take some exercises that are related to visionary thinking and a curious open mind.

A friend suggests having your wedding in complete darkness. No lights at all. Postpone making up your mind as to whether you like the idea or not. Think up only potential positive consequences for this idea. Next, think up only potential negative consequences for this idea. And finally, think up potential alternative ideas that would lead to the same positive consequences without the same negative consequences.

You have heard about a new car manufacturer that puts square wheels on their cars. Don't have an attitude toward this idea. Look for potential interesting perspectives for cars with square wheels.

A friend suggests restricting your internet and email access to ten minutes per day. Postpone making up your mind as to whether you like the idea or not. Think up only potential positive consequences for this idea. Next, think up only potential negative consequences for this idea. And finally, think up potential alternative ideas that would lead to the same positive consequences without the same negative consequences.

You hear about a new café serving coffee in tin cans. You need to open your coffee using a can opener. Don't have an attitude toward this idea. Look for potential interesting perspectives for coffee served in tin cans.

A friend suggests replacing "eating at the dinner table" with "walking dinners" for your everyday evening meal. Never again will you sit down for dinner. Postpone making up your mind as to whether you like the idea or not. Think up only potential positive consequences for this idea. Next, think up only potential negative consequences for this idea. And finally, think up potential alternative ideas that would lead to the same positive consequences without the same negative consequences.

You hear about a new trend where people put their televisions in their bathrooms. No more television in the living room or in the bedrooms. Don't have an attitude toward this idea. Look for potential interesting perspectives for only having televisions in bathrooms.

Practicing persuasion

Finally, let's do some exercises that are related to persuasive idea presentations.

Imagine a doctor's waiting room designed as a small movie theater. The patients will watch short videos about health, diseases, and nutrition while waiting to see the doctor. Think of a possible gatekeeper for this idea, such as a leader of a company, doctor, friend, colleague, influencer, or your wife or husband. Make a persuasive message that presents this idea to the gatekeeper as a poster, email, PowerPoint presentation, video script, elevator pitch, etc.

Imagine a punching bag shaped as a human. It comes with a variety of "villain costumes" so you can dress it up as the Joker (from Batman), Darth Vader (from Star Wars), etc. Come up with some persuasive illustrations and catchphrases for this idea.

Imagine a pedestrian crossing where pedestrians waiting to cross the road are video recorded and projected onto the road in front of the cars driving toward the crossing. Think of a possible gatekeeper for this idea, such as a leader of a company, head of the technical department in a municipality, friend, colleague, influencer, or your wife or husband. Make a persuasive message that presents this idea to the gatekeeper as a poster, email, PowerPoint presentation, video script, elevator pitch, etc.

Imagine edible napkins and wipes. You can use them to wipe off food around your mouth and eat them afterward. They are healthy. Come up with some persuasive illustrations and catchphrases for this idea.

Imagine a new restaurant concept where the menu card is replaced by a "welcome plate" from which you can try a small taste of every dish from the menu. Afterward, you order the dish you like best. Think of a possible gatekeeper for this idea, such as a leader of a company, a restaurant owner, friend, colleague, influencer, your wife, or husband. Make a persuasive message that presents this idea to the gatekeeper as a poster, email, PowerPoint presentation, video script, elevator pitch, etc.

Imagine a refrigerator that releases a horrible smell when you open the refrigerator door outside eating hours. This will stop you from eating snacks all day. Come up with some persuasive illustrations and catchphrases for this idea.

Professional Exercises

Ready to do some creativity exercises based on professional problem areas? This type of creativity exercise seems more serious because they simulate real problems from your work.

They are not more effective in advancing your creative skills or boosting your creative confidence. Not more effective than exercises based on everyday problem areas. In fact, you may need to make an extra effort simulating the "sandbox" environment for your practice sessions. Too many exercises based on professional problem areas can make the entire practice feel a bit too serious. Practicing creativity needs a to be playful. It needs to be relaxed and fun. It needs to be a safe place to think up, share, and elaborate on wild ideas.

However, professional problem areas can help legitimize your creativity fitness center toward otherwise reluctant team members. Try to think about them as a second step of your creativity practice. Everyday problem areas help to give your creative confidence a quick boost. Professional problem areas take your practice closer to real work problems.

Step one: Exercises not related to your work. Step two: Exercises simulating work-related problem areas. Step three: Integrating creativity into your real and personal work tasks.

The key is to identify situations that simulate problems related to your profession and industry. Do you work in sales? Then you will need to identify all kinds of problem areas related to sales. What could be an interesting target for your creativity? What do you wish you had time to work on creatively? Which of your previous problems could be interesting to revisit with some dedicated creative efforts? Turn these professional problem areas into creativity exercises for your practice.

Which professional problem areas to choose? You can bring practically any professional problem into your creativity fitness center. But make sure that every member of your team will instantly recognize and understand the problem areas.

Lengthy problem descriptions tend to have a diminishing effect on creative efforts. Can you describe the problem in less than five sentences? Perfect! Need a full page to describe the problem? Skip the problem. Find another professional situation to use for your exercise.

You may choose professional problem areas that are not directly related to your own team. Problems that are universal for your profession. Or fundamental problems that may appear across industries. You may think your problems are uniquely yours. However, some problem areas are universal. Teams face some overlapping problems regardless of their industry. Universal problems may relate to internal team communication, sharing of team experiences, team meetings, decision-making, introduction of new technologies, development of a team culture, and optimizing work processes.

Let's go through a few examples of problems that may be relevant for your professional creativity exercises.

For exploration and problem understanding, you may choose to challenge the traditional way of kick-starting a meeting, or to challenge your team's calendar system. You may also choose to generate problem definitions related to email handling or hybrid meetings.

For imagination and idea production, you may choose to look for new ways to digitalize a specific work task or visualize each team member's workload. You may also choose to produce ideas for reducing disruptions in open office spaces or for improving the onboarding of newly hired team members.

For visionary idea evaluation, you may simulate a 24-hour right of withdrawal for decision-making. That in order to make better decisions, your colleague suggests introducing a 24-hour right of withdrawal (cancellation) for all decisions made during meetings. Or to simulate a colleague suggesting that nobody would be allowed to stay in their team role for more than two years. That every two years, everyone would switch roles and responsibilities. Or even simulate that for the next two years, you would only promote and hire female candidates for future jobs.

For persuasive idea presentations, you may make use of ideas coming up during exercises where you challenge standards in your profession and where you imagine new ideas for professional problem areas. Develop persuasive presentations for these ideas.

Other types of problems also seem to go across industries. They are like mirrored problem areas. They mirror problems on a principal level. Let's go back to the problems related to a supermarket checkout situation. Making people form lines—this seems to be a problem lots of teams are facing. Putting products onto a flat surface. Moving objects on a belt. Scanning. Payment. Providing a good customer experience. These are also problems that lots of teams are facing across industries.

Having a cross-professional team? No problem. In fact, good for you. Most likely, you will still be able to identify problem areas that everyone will instantly recognize and understand. If not, split your team into smaller groups with separate creativity fitness programs to match their professions and work.

Societal Exercises

There is a third type of creativity exercises for your creativity fitness center. They are based on societal problem areas. History has shown how people are fascinated by problems that go beyond everyday life and professional work. How we want to understand the world; want to change the world. Make it a better place. How we want to make a mark on history. These problems can awaken a deeply rooted human energy. This makes such problems perfect for your creativity exercising. Consider them as inspiring add-ons. Like extra cream for your cake.

Societal problem areas are more challenging. They require big thinking. They may be too difficult in the early period of your creativity practice. But they are perfect add-ons in the later stages. As professional exercises become too easy, you can spice up the fitness center with some societal problem areas.

Societal problem areas may relate to local communities, cultural groups, nations, world regions, or the entire world. You may challenge the handling of immigration in your local community. You may try to come up with ideas for how minority groups can better express their point of view, or open-mindedly visualize perspectives from "national enemies".

Societal problem areas can also relate to science, art, and political matters. You may challenge standard ideas for how it all started. Challenge standard ideas for why diversity exists within and between species. You could also try to come up with ideas that may explain why humans produce tears when we cry. Try visualizing an alien completely different from any historical, living, and fictitious species from planet earth. Visualize how it moves, eats, breathes, communicates, fights, and sleeps. Or try categorizing species into completely new categories. It is all about coming up with big questions that fascinate you and your team.

Four-Phase Creativity Journey

I once worked with a global human development department in a large multinational company. They were responsible for key competence development programs for the entire organization. This included training of leaders and employees from sourcing, logistics, production, packaging, marketing, sales, distribution, service, finance, accounting, management, and business development.

They wanted to develop a new training program on creativity. One that could offer more than simple tools and process methods. One that could lead to real innovative changes in everyday work tasks and innovative projects. That could help take their teams on a creativity journey to become far more innovative.

We designed a cross-organizational, four-phase creativity journey. It was possible to start a creativity journey as an individual or as an entire team.

The first phase was preparation. A preparation for the journey, and an introduction to the journey. The preparation phase was designed to create a common language and understanding about creativity. To set expectations and stimulate motivation for the following three phases of the creativity journey. For individuals, this phase was conducted via an online-learning platform, involving a series of instruction and demonstration videos as well as several self-instructed practical exercises and reflection tasks. For teams, this phase was conducted as an instructor-led face-to-face seminar or as a virtual workshop.

The second phase was the development of creative confidence. It was designed as shorter daily creative practice sessions or as longer weekly sessions. If possible, the practice was planned in the morning to create direct spillover effects into the rest of the workday. For teams, the practice was mostly conducted as face-to-face sessions in standard meeting rooms. For individuals, the practice was conducted in a virtual cross-organizational community. All practice was organized into groups of three to four to reduce fear of judgment and to avoid free-rider problems.

The third phase was to support the integration of creative efforts into everyday work tasks. This support included facilitated creativity meetings and workshops as well as facilitated creativity sessions as part of existing problem-solving methods in the organization, such as LEAN and Design Thinking. The informal integration was supported by suggestions, discussions, and reflections on how to get into creative mode during everyday work tasks. The cross-organizational practice community turned into a community of practice. Members could bring their real work problems and solve them in collaboration with the community.

The fourth phase was to set expectations for creativity. During phases two and three, the participants had gained relevant creative skills. They knew how to be creative when asked to be creative. They had gained stronger creative confidence. They were confident that they could successfully come up with creative solutions for complex problems. It was now possible to set serious expectations for creative efforts.

Want to upgrade your engine for innovation? To kick-start your creativity journey?

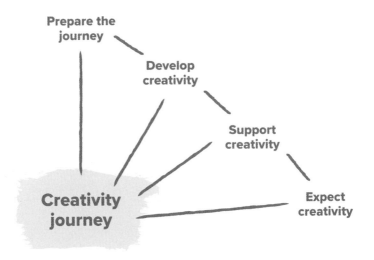

Let's take a deep dive into how you can plan the four phases of your creativity journey.

Phase 1: Prepare the Journey

You have decided to get started. Now, let's make it a five-star journey. Preparation is the first step.

Your first reflections should be concerned about what to practice. Which creative skills and confidence do you need? You may start off examining your creative efforts, creative self-perception, and your creative team culture. Are you satisfied with your current creative efforts? Do you consider yourself highly creative? Do you have a culture of originality? Is there room for improvement? What are your innovative ambitions? Which creative skills are important to you?

Need more alternative ideas? More novel ideas? More valuable ideas? Start practicing your imagination. Start practicing how to identify interesting new connections for idea combinations; to make fearless elaborations on novel ideas.

Need a more curious open mind toward new ideas? To look for potential where others only find trouble? Start practicing your visionary mindset. Start practicing how to look for alternative explanations; disciplining your mind during idea evaluation. Postpone making up your mind while looking for potential in new ideas.

Need more ambitious innovative challenges? Do you want to upgrade your innovative ambition to include curiosity-driven problem-solving? Start practicing how to challenge what everyone else takes for granted. Explore more alternative, well-defined sub-problems. Identify high innovation potential problems that are more motivating and interesting to work on.

Need support for your novel ideas? To win over gatekeepers more effectively? To make your audiences accept or comply with your new ideas? Start practicing persuasion. Preparing persuasive idea presentations. Making use of effective means of persuasion pointing toward the key value of your novel ideas.

Your second reflection should be concerned about who needs practice. What functions, decisions, or work processes need more creativity? What type of problems need creative solutions? Those people directly related to these problems may need a boost of creative confidence.

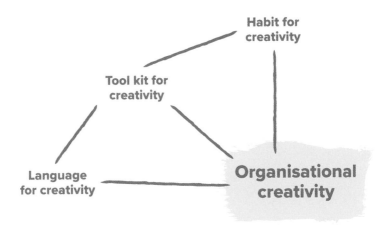

Not everyone may need their creativity to become second nature, but you may need to develop a common language about creativity for everyone in your organization. Categorize your organization into the following three groups:

A: Those who need to understand the benefits and purpose of creativity, such as a language for creativity.

B: Those who need a tool kit to temporarily enhance creativity during meetings and workshops.

C: Those who need a new habit of creativity, so it comes naturally to them whenever creativity is needed.

Do you have a long list of participants? Then think about your journey in terms of waves. The first wave of participants should be based on voluntary commitment. Find a voluntary team. Or find a group of dedicated participants from across several teams. Participants who immediately recognize the rationale of the creativity journey. Sign them up for your creativity fitness center. Make their journey a first-class experience. Use this group to create a positive awareness about the creativity journey across your organization. Let the first wave help motivate new participants for the second wave. Design your fitness center to take in employees and leaders in consecutive or overlapping waves.

Should the leaders join the creativity fitness center? Yes. In order to understand the creativity journey, they need to try it out for themselves. To support creative efforts better, to set meaningful expectations for creative efforts, and to be creative themselves. To be creative about leadership problems. And to be creative with their employees on all other sorts of problems.

Leaders may need to practice creativity in a separate wave. It may make sense to let them be a part of the first wave in the fitness center. This way, they will advance their creativity before employees start their journey. This will allow leaders to play a key role in making the entire creativity journey a success. It will also give them a chance to prepare for how to manage and lead employees well as they boost their creative confidence. Do you have a flat, hierarchical structure? Yes. Then it may make better sense to let leaders join waves together with employees.

Now, you can start developing the creativity exercises for your fitness center. Exercises based on everyday problem areas are no problem. The same goes for exercises based on societal problem areas. However, the exercises based on professional problem areas are critical.

You now know what creative skills to practice. You also know who will join the practice. There may be several professions involved in the practice. Thus, you need to design professional exercises that match these professions. That simulate daily work tasks for the participants in your fitness center. You may need to consider this as you create the groups for each wave. Maybe each wave could have their own set of exercises. Specifically adjusted to the profession and work of each group.

It may be a good idea to develop some of the exercises as your creativity journey unfolds. Participants can even help suggest relevant professional problem areas to include in creativity exercises as they learn the logic of this type of exercise. Participants first need to learn the logic of the exercises by trying them out. So make sure you have exercises for at least the first few weeks of practice.

Your third reflection should be concerned about how to kick-start the creativity journey. Participants will need to understand the rationale and the practicalities of the creativity fitness center. They need an introduction to the exercises and expectations for the practice.

There are lots of interesting formats for such an introduction, such as workshops, seminars, booklets, videos, info-meetings, intranet messages, emails, a dedicated website, or an app. Prepare yourself well for delivering the introduction. The preparation is particularly important if the introduction is a live workshop or seminar.

Make sure the introduction includes a killer sales pitch. You may find some inspiration from this book to prepare your introduction. However, the introduction should be directly related to your organizational strategy.

Maybe your strategy includes a stronger focus on innovation. Try this: Creativity is the engine for innovation.

Do you have a strategy about diversity and inclusion? Creativity also has a strong link to diversity and inclusion. **A curious, open mind is naturally more inclusive.** Odd perspectives are a positive thing for creativity. Homogeneity can hinder teams from developing new ideas. You need diversity to get more interesting new connections for your idea combinations.

Does your team need some serious team building? The creativity journey lets you experience a new side of your colleagues. It lets you experience how you are all creative human beings. You can see more potential in your colleagues after having experienced how they come up with interesting ideas. How they are open-minded toward your novel ideas. How they help elaborate your novel ideas. You learn how to have fun while being seriously creative together on important and complex problems.

Do you have a strategy to increase psychological safety and social wellbeing? Creativity can lead to higher internal motivation for work tasks involving creative efforts.

What should your killer pitch be based upon? Put some effort into this introduction.

Phase 2: Develop Creativity

I once worked with an international soft-drink producer. They already had effective idea systems in place for collecting, evaluating, and implementing ideas suggested by employees and leaders from across the organization. Most ideas were highly feasible; almost too feasible. Novel ideas were rarely suggested in their idea system. They wanted to increase the number of novel ideas. They wanted employees and leaders to be able to come up with more of those wild ideas. To dare sharing these ideas in the idea system.

They designed an app-based weekly creativity practice program. Each team would have three weekly exercises. Two exercises based on everyday problem areas. And one exercise based on professional problem areas. The professional exercises were designed as company challenges. They simulated bigger challenges related to specific departments in the company. They were defined so that everyone, regardless of their profession, would instantly understand the challenge. As a continual reminder, these weekly challenges were also put up as posters in the hallways.

The practice was conducted in smaller groups. The groups were encouraged to upload their ideas into the idea system on the app as short video presentations or as text descriptions. Rewards, such as restaurant vouchers, were given to groups that uploaded surprisingly novel ideas.

In another context, I worked with a partnership of universities developing an online gamified creativity fitness center. It was designed for young university students and included both an avatar, instant feedback points, progress badges, and an elaborate storyline.

I have also worked in projects developing creativity fitness centers based on virtual communication software such as Microsoft Teams and Zoom. However, most creativity fitness centers are based on face-to-face practice taking place in meeting rooms, conference rooms, or innovation laboratories.

What should your creativity fitness center be like? Should it be app-based? Web-based? In a physical room? If you go for shorter daily practice sessions, you will need to have a fitness center that is local or virtual. Participants should not have to walk ten minutes to have a fifteen-minute practice session. Longer weekly practice sessions provide the possibility of creating dedicated physical spaces that stimulate creativity during the practice.

You don't have a creativity room? No problem. It can basically be any room. If possible, find a room that you can dedicate to creativity and innovation. A room that can be used for the practice as well as for all other creative and innovative efforts. Make sure the room is unique. It must have a distinct interior and decor. It must be different from your other rooms.

The participants will get lots of creative experiences in this specific room. These experiences will create an emotional, cognitive, and social connection between the room and your creative efforts in the room. Going to the room will be associated with a special way of thinking and a special way of being together. A creative way. A creative connection. As the connection grows stronger, it will act like a trigger for your creative mode. You will find it easier to get into the creative mode as you enter this room.

You may have noticed how modes of thinking and behavior change depending on the room you enter. You rarely find a lot of energized dialogue during lectures in large university auditoriums. You may find it easier to talk about private matters in a bar than in a church. You may be fine about nudity in a sauna, but you may never accept the same level of nudity at your workplace. You have unwritten rules related to different types of rooms and places. The creativity journey is an opportunity to write some rules of engagement for a special creativity or innovation room in your organization.

Be aware that shorter daily sessions have a higher likelihood of a daily spillover effect compared to what you see with weekly sessions. Daily exercising will constantly bring the participants back to the creative mode. This makes it more likely that the creative way of thinking and interacting will have a positive effect on other work tasks that occur immediately after the daily practice sessions. However, it may be easier to plan for weekly sessions, especially if your participants come from several teams located apart from each other.

Try to integrate the practice sessions as naturally as possible into your daily or weekly schedule. Maybe you already have daily morning meetings. Or maybe you have a weekly status meeting. Place the creativity practice in connection with these meetings. You don't have any daily or weekly meetings relevant for your group of participants? Then maybe you can identify some other types of daily or weekly routines that the practice can be related to.

Participants will need instructions during each practice session. You may develop written instruction cards, short instruction videos, or you may have an instructor demonstrating and explaining the exercises for each session. Make the instructions short and clear. Participants should not spend their time discussing what to do. They should instantly be able to start the creativity exercise.

At your kick-start workshop, you may be able to identify one or two highly motivated participants. They could be given a role of coordination and instruction for the entire group. Or maybe you have some organizational process facilitators. It may be good practice for them to instruct these creative practice sessions. Maybe they can use this instructor experience for future facilitation of creative and innovative efforts.

Few participants will be able to participate in all practice sessions. Due to sickness, holidays, and urgent work matters, participants may need to cancel one or more practice sessions. You may be able to reduce the number of cancellations by creating fixed weekly or monthly practice groups. Being in the same practice group for a longer period will create a higher level of commitment. You will know the others are waiting for you at the practice session. Because of this, participants will attempt to reschedule their practice rather than simply cancel it.

The practice groups should not be fixed for the entire practice period. Mix up the practice groups as often as possible. This will allow the participants to experience more of their colleagues creatively. They will become more confident with their creativity in different social contexts. They will develop creative skills and confidence in relation to all kinds of people.

Creativity is fun. Being creative with colleagues is an exciting experience. However, the initial excitement for the creativity exercises will slowly wear off. That doesn't mean that the participants don't like creativity anymore. But maybe you can spice up the creativity practice with some new types of exercises. Come up with some new, inspiring everyday problem areas. Find more motivating professional problem areas. And include societal problem areas that are based on the participants' personal interests.

There may be other ways you can freshen up the creativity practice.

You could introduce a round of a "creativity memory game" to the practice. In normal memory games, you have several illustrated cards faced down. Players turn over two cards. Two identical cards are a match, and the player gets a point. If the cards are not identical, the player must turn the cards back over again. The game continues until all cards are matched. The player with the most points wins. The key is to remember the cards that are turned back facing down.

In the "creativity memory game," there are no identical cards. The cards illustrate random objects, professions, and organizations. The cards are faced down. You turn over two cards. You now have sixty seconds to combine the objects, professions, or organizations illustrated on the two cards. Develop new ideas from these combinations. Present three new ideas before the time is up and you get a point. Ideas are new if they are new to the participants in your practice group. If you don't make it in sixty seconds, you must turn the cards back over again. The game continues until all cards are turned into points. The player with the most points wins. The key is to practice making interesting, new connections between objects, professions, and organizations.

You could also introduce a round of a "creativity race-to-win game" to the practice. In most race-to-win games, players move a game piece from start to finish on a game board. Players throw dice. The number shown on the dice indicates how many moves you can go forward. The game continues until one or all players get to finish. The game is largely based on luck and simple logical strategies.

In the "creativity race-to-win game," there are no dice. You must still get from start to finish on a game board. The winner is still the first to finish. You will need a deck of cards with pictures of random everyday and work-related problem areas. You pick a random card from the deck. You now have sixty seconds to identify problems related to the pictured situation. And to produce new ideas for these identified problems. Ideas are new if they are new to the participants in your practice group. The number of new ideas tells how many moves you can go forward. Two ideas allow two moves forward. Six ideas allow six moves forward. The game is largely based on problem exploration and idea production.

Take any other game. Replace existing game activities with relevant creative efforts. Make the creative efforts part of how you win the game. Now you've got a fun and fresh new exercise for your creativity practice.

Phase 3: Support Creativity

Your creative skills are growing stronger. Your creative confidence is getting better. It's now time to support creative efforts outside the fitness center.

Eventually, participants will start an informal integration of their new creative skills and confidence. Some participants will quickly get creative about all sorts of everyday work tasks. They will start to integrate creativity whenever creativity is needed. It will come relatively easy for them to identify when and where to apply some creativity. Others will need more time for this. They will need support to succeed in making full use of their new creative skills and confidence.

Participants will find it easier to be creative in smaller groups. They will find it easier to be creative with participants from the creativity fitness center, easier to be creative individually, easier to be creative on problems they personally find important. Easier to be creative on informal work tasks. However, they will need support integrating creativity in bigger groups, during formal work tasks, and for problems that may not be considered important to the individual but may be important for the whole team.

Support for creativity is about putting structure into creativity. Where to invest your creative efforts? Can you develop some formal procedures for creativity to apply when creativity is needed? Can you define the types of problems that should trigger these procedures? What type of problems, situations, or ideas should set off these resources? What kind of support do you need from management and colleagues to succeed with your creative efforts? What does it take for you to put some serious creative effort into relevant work tasks?

It may be worth organizing a seminar for discussing how your creativity support system should be designed. You will need a strong commitment from leaders to set up your support system. Make sure they participate in this seminar and that they will be involved in the daily support for creativity. The seminar can easily overlap with your continuous practice in the creativity fitness center. You don't need to finish the entire practice program before you start integrating creativity into formal and informal work tasks.

Most participants will be positive toward this phase of the creativity journey. They will have felt how the creativity exercises fostered positive and energetic experiences with their colleagues. They may expect that creativity can have the same effect during daily work tasks. However, you may also have a few participants who consider this phase challenging. They cannot clearly see how creativity can become a meaningful part of their daily work tasks. They may argue how they are "here to work, not to be creative." They will need some extra support figuring out how creative efforts may benefit their work specifically.

Some types of work have obvious benefits from creativity. Other types of work may have fewer and less obvious benefits from creativity. However, during my fifteen years of applied research and consultancy involving more than one hundred thousand professionals from across almost all kinds of industries, I have yet to see a type of work that has no potential benefits from creativity.

You may need to define specific work tasks for which creativity should be integrated. It may also include the development of a process method for how to be creative on these work tasks. Do you already have a detailed problem-solving method? Maybe you could update this method to include some creative efforts. Or you could develop a more creative version of your current problem-solving method. Then you will have two versions: one for standard problem-solving and another for creative problem-solving.

Your support for creativity may also include the formation of a creativity squad. The squad may offer facilitation of creativity meetings and innovative workshops. It may also offer other kinds of help for doing problem understanding, idea production, idea evaluation, and idea presentation. The team may temporarily join projects involving complex problem-solving as well as projects with high ambitions for innovation. As such, they become like a new profession in your organization—professional idea machines.

The creativity squad could develop an idea system for collecting and evaluating new ideas as well as contributing to the implementing of novel ideas. This will make it easier to identify and succeed with novel ideas from across the entire organization.

The squad could be made up of a few part-time employees who are positive toward creativity. Or it could be made up of several full-time highly creative leaders and employees. Maybe you already have some creative colleagues in mind? Could they be up for taking a key role for supporting creativity in your organization?

Maybe you can support the most novel ideas with a Kickstarter package. A Kickstarter package with just enough resources to test a novel idea. To quickly learn more about idea feasibility and desirability. A Kickstarter package could include a small amount of money as well as some dedicated work hours and counselling.

How far should this go? How many work tasks need creativity? Do you need creativity everywhere? The burning question is whether you want creativity to become an integrated part of your daily schedule. Should creativity be part of your way of working? Your organizational DNA? Do you want creativity to become like a habit for most of your teams? Or do you want creativity to become something extraordinary, separated from your way of working? Everyone may need some level of creativity. But some select few may be responsible for taking creativity to a higher level. Do you need creativity distributed evenly across your organization? Or do specific teams need creativity more than others? Who should receive the most support for creativity?

Phase 4: Expect Creativity

You now have creative skills. You have gained creative confidence. You have designed structures for supporting creativity. Everyone knows where to invest their creative efforts. Everyone knows how to be creative. You can be creative at will. You can be creative on command.

Now you can start setting expectations for creativity. You may even define some key performance indicators related to creativity.

Do you have an organizational culture with no performance indicators? Then it may not make sense to introduce specific performance indicators related to creativity.

Do you have clear performance indicators across your organization? Then you may need some indicators directly related to creativity to send clear signals about your expectations for creative efforts.

You may set expectations in terms of creative performance. This could be set up as a system for capturing new ideas. A physical idea board. Or a digital idea board. How many ideas do you expect per employee or per team every month? Maybe you can post monthly creative challenges and set expectations for everyone to contribute with at least twenty alternative ideas. Or at least two novel ideas. Such creative performance may be part of determining who will be the employee of the month.

Another approach for creative performance expectations is directed toward higher ambitions for innovation. Expect that all employees and leaders start up a project based on curiosity-driven problem-solving. A personal professional creative effort. It should be based on their own individual curiosity. What they find interesting. What they believe is important to solve with some novel solutions. This can help set new standards in your organization and industry. You may include an expectation for how much time each employee and leader should invest in their curiosity-driven project. Set expectations for how many hours per month. For example, tell them to allocate two hours per month or per week. Or tell them to spend 5% or 20% of their time dedicated to this project, looking for new, innovative possibilities.

They will need to work on a problem of their interest. Otherwise, it's hard to make it curiosity-driven. They may choose problems that you don't consider urgent for your organization. You may ask them for a rationale for their choice to understand and guide their choices better. However, you may need to trust their curiosity. They may have some insights you don't have. They may have seen a problem that your organization will face in the near future. A problem that may become urgent soon, unless it's handled now. Curiosity-driven problem-solving helps you solve such problems before they turn into burning platforms.

One may be curious about how to rethink meeting structures. Another may be curious about how to optimize a specific machine in the production. A third may be more curious about how to improve your products or services. A fourth may want to challenge the way you conduct interviews with job applicants. Some may have overlapping interests. This allows them to work together and combine their creative efforts.

It may feel a bit messy with all those diverse innovative projects. However, their curiosity drive will ensure a stronger creative motivation and a stronger creative perseverance. Curiosity is a powerful driver of creative efforts. Remember to think about creative efforts as investments in your future. How much are you willing to invest in your future?

You may reward creative efforts with some recognition. Maybe a diploma for each great idea. An award for continuous creative efforts on a complex problem. Or a bonus for each attempt to implement a novel idea.

Do you want even more and better creativity? Set expectations for leaders to sustain and further develop creativity. Leaders need to communicate how creativity must be prioritized. This will help those employees who really like creativity. It will help them keep the spirit high, help them win over those who may, at first, be hesitant toward creativity.

Ask leaders to conduct an annual team questionnaire and discussion examining the state of the creative culture, creative efforts, and creative self-perception. Ask them to follow up with an action plan to handle potential issues related to creativity.

Let leaders demonstrate how they continuously nurture creativity in their teams. Let them present which problems their teams are currently investing their creative efforts to solve. Let them provide examples of novel ideas developed and implemented by their teams. This will also help inspire other teams in your organization.

Do you want to set expectations for creativity during everyday situations? Start asking your colleagues and leaders to contribute their creativity.

"Can I hear about your other ideas? What other ideas did you consider before falling in love with this idea?"

"Remember to set aside time for creativity. Remember to go for lots of alternative ideas; for novel ideas."

"Please, surprise me. Bring me some ideas that are different from all your previous ideas."

"Let's agree to have a minimum of forty alternative ideas before we start evaluating any of them."

"Can you show me all the positive perspectives you identified about your alternative ideas? What was interesting about the ideas that you decided to reject?"

"Can you tell me about your creative efforts? What did you do? How did you do it? Who was involved? How did you ensure a serious creative effort to solve this problem?"

Final Words

It is an honor for me that you've taken your time to read this book.

I hope this book has given you some inspiring insights into how you can explore new grounds, imagine new ideas, make visionary idea evaluations, and prepare persuasive idea presentations.

More importantly, I hope this book triggered a motivation to kick-start your own creativity journey. A creativity journey that can help turn you into a more successful innovator.

Problems are a natural part of your everyday life. You are born to handle all sorts of problems. You are good at solving problems you know well, using solutions you have tried before. However, as problems become more complex, you may feel unsure about what to do. As the solution space becomes uncertain, you may hesitate to do something about your problems. You may try to ignore the complex problems, hoping they will somehow disappear on their own.

Unsolved complex problems may lead to worry and anxiety. You may end up viewing complex problems as something negative. Something you try to avoid. This causes a circular effect where your unsolved problems increase stress levels, and the higher levels of stress make it difficult to handle even the simplest of your problems.

As a creative, you are far more at ease solving complex problems. Creativity empowers you to solve complex problems like they are nothing special. It brings a lot of fun into your creative efforts. It leads to higher levels of motivation for solving your problems. Creativity makes it feel like you are eating problems for breakfast.

I am constantly trying to develop better and more effective means for advancing creative skills and boosting creative confidence. You can always find my newest creativity tool kits and a catalog of creativity exercises on my website. Most of it is free to download. You are also welcome to join my Idea Club. It's free. You will find it all at www.ChristianByrge.com

The time has now come for you to make some serious decisions. When will you start your creativity journey? Which creative skill are you going to turn into a powerful new habit? And who will you take with you on this journey?

I wish you all the best on your creativity journey!

Best wishes,
PhD Christian Byrge

About the Author

As an internationally recognized scholar, Christian Byrge has delivered creativity training to more than 100,000 professionals from world-leading organizations across most industries in Europe, Asia, and America. He has advised more than 300 organizations on how to develop creativity as a team culture, as an effective work process, and as a set of powerful leadership and employee skills.

For more than 17 years, Christian has been studying how to regain and further develop innovative skills and creative confidence. His achievements include a long list of impactful scientific and practitioner-oriented publications, as well as several internationally recognized tool kits for advancing and enhancing creativity for individuals and teams.

Please visit Christian Byrge's website to learn more about his research, his publications, and his tool kits: www.ChristianByrge.com